Wildlife Walkabouts

1. Avo d Somerset Border

8 ected by

WAYSIDE BOOKS
CLEVEDON, AVON

British Library Cataloguing in Publication Data

Woods, Michael, *1948*-
Avon and Somerset border.—(Wildlife walkabouts; 1)
1. Somerset—Description and travel—Guide-books
2. Avon—Description and travel—Guide-books
I. Title II. Series
914.23 804858 DA670.S5

ISBN 0-948264-00-4

First published in 1985 by
Wayside Books,
3 Park Road, Clevedon, Avon BS21 7JG

Design and maps by Ralph Sandoe

Typeset by Wayside Graphics, Clevedon, Avon
Printed by Colourways Press Ltd, Clevedon, Avon
Bound by W. H. Ware & Son Ltd, Clevedon, Avon

*To the publisher's children,
Clare and Alexandra, and, naturally,
to the Woods.*

Acknowledgements

This book would not have been possible without help from the following people – my father, Doug Woods; Chris and Mary Potts; Alec Coles and Jane Evans; John Boyd; Janet Gardner; Julia Morland for her fine illustrations and Ralph Sandoe who conceived and produced the project – to each and everyone of you, thank you.

Publisher's Note

It is hoped that this book, if successful, is to be the first of a series entitled *Wildlife Walkabouts*. With this in mind the publisher welcomes any constructive criticism or praise from readers on any aspect of this publication. Please write to the publisher, or author, at Wayside Books, 3 Park Road, Clevedon, Avon BS21 7JG.

Where the routes of these eight walks cross farmland, as far as could be ascertained they follow public footpaths which were in existence at the time of going to press. No responsibility can be taken by the author or the publisher for any errors which may lead to action being taken against readers and users of this book.

CONTENTS

LIST OF ILLUSTRATIONS IN TEXT

INTRODUCTION

In this book you will find the routes of eight short walks together with a wide range of information about the things you may see when following them. The walks have been deliberately selected to do two things. They are all very different in terrain, in habitat and, most important, in the variety of wildlife you will come across. They avoid, as far as possible, existing nature trails and areas of particular importance for the rare species they contain. If you are lucky enough to come across an unusual orchid or a rare bird, that is very much your good fortune; I have not led you there for that purpose although I may, perhaps, have opened your eyes to your surroundings on the way.

I have not restricted the walks to any particular season, so a few of the species I have mentioned may not be around during your visit. On the other hand, you will probably spot some not included in the text that were not to be found when I was there.

Wildlife habitats are a diminishing resource in a countryside under pressure from agricultural intensification, afforestation, urbanisation and road building. Yet there is an increasing interest in natural history and a growing number of people go into the countryside to relax, to find peace, and to pursue their hobbies.

I hope the walks described in this book will enhance those trips and may even introduce you to some new areas. Perhaps you will also find the book good to read beside a roaring fire on a dark winter's evening when the swallows are long gone and the scent of new-mown grass is a dimming memory.

Michael Woods

Notes

Wood pigeons
Rooks
Birch
Heron
Swans
Willow
Mallard
Kingfisher
Bulrush
Teasel
Goldfinch on burdock
Moorhens
Hare

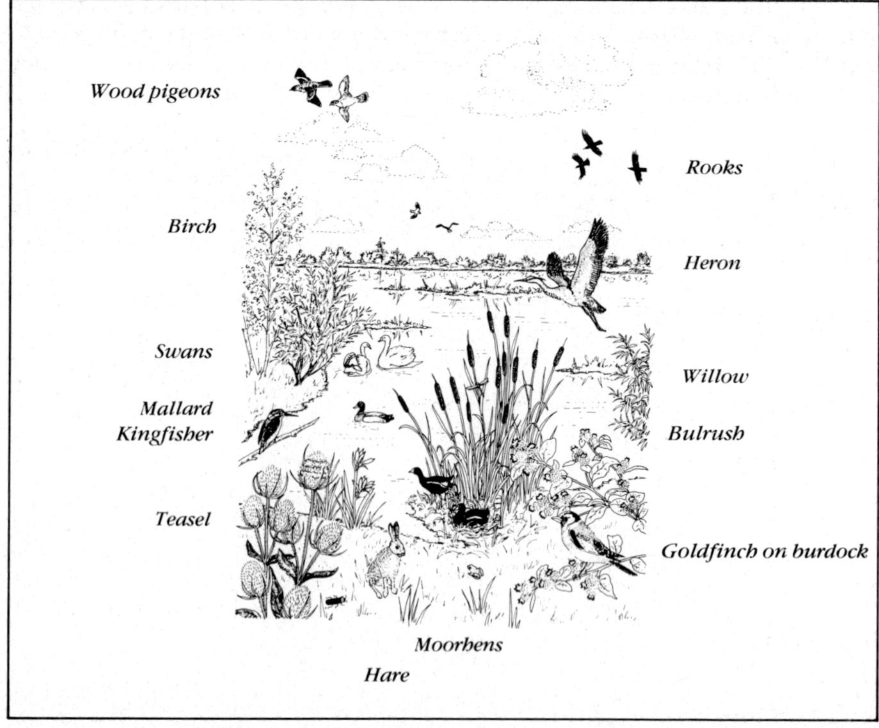

Westhay Moor

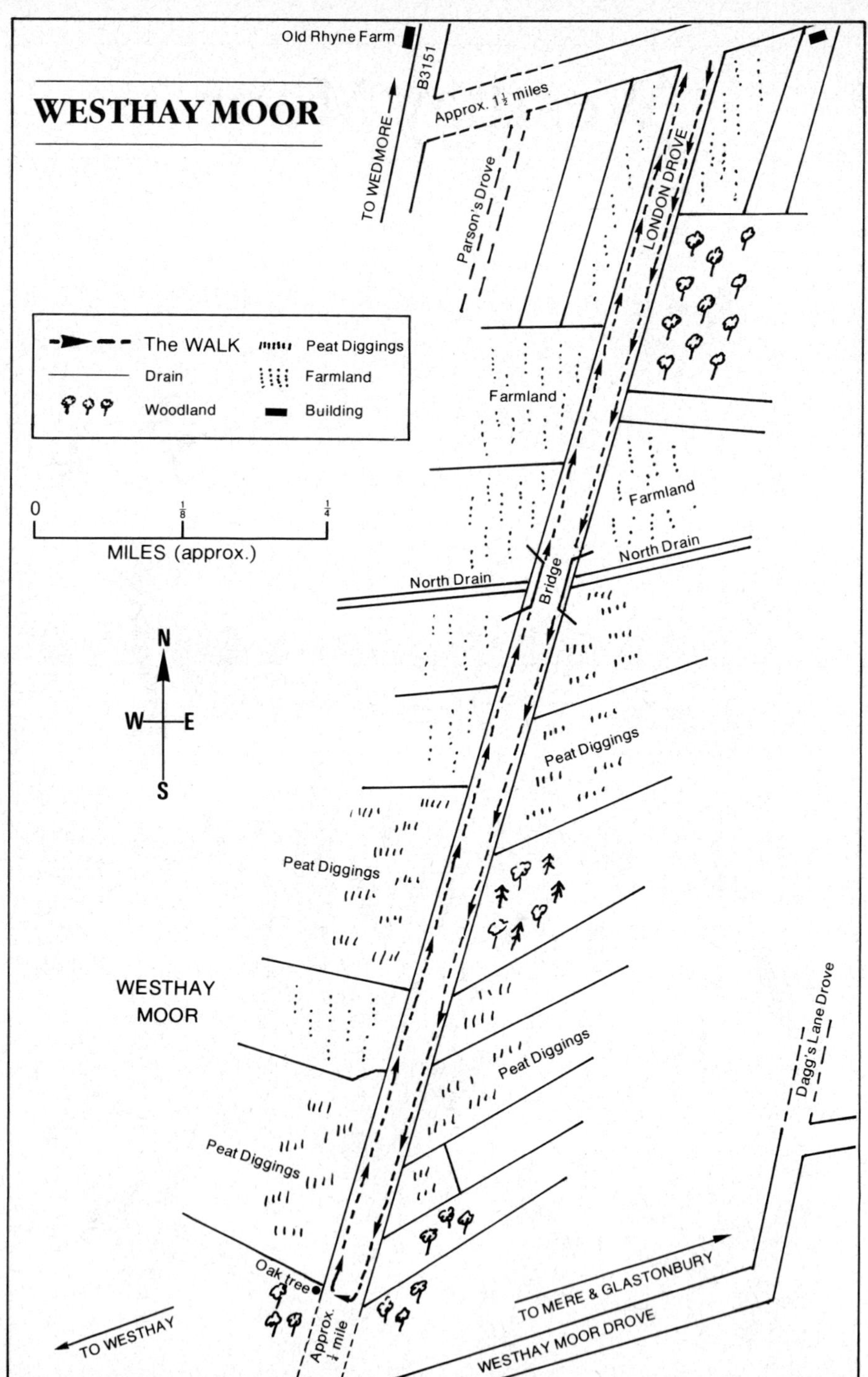
WESTHAY MOOR
Old Rhyne Farm
B3151
TO WEDMORE
Approx. 1½ miles
Parson's Drove
LONDON DROVE
The WALK
Drain
Woodland
Peat Diggings
Farmland
Building
Farmland
Farmland
0
⅛
¼
MILES (approx.)
North Drain
North Drain
Bridge
N
W
E
S
Peat Diggings
Peat Diggings
WESTHAY
MOOR
Peat Diggings
Peat Diggings
Dagg's Lane Drove
Oak tree
Approx. ¼ mile
TO WESTHAY
TO MERE & GLASTONBURY
WESTHAY MOOR DROVE

WESTHAY MOOR O.S. ST44(454453) – A flat walk along a drove

Anyone living on the hills surrounding the Levels will know how frequently this area is shrouded in mist; a thin layer of white cloud with the dark skeletal forms of trees protruding through it. To venture into that mist is an eerie experience. It is a silent clammy world where stock move as quiet ghostly figures; grey shapes on a grey ground, looming in and out of sight. Pigeons may crash out of trees at your approach or perhaps a heron with a loud 'fraank' will take to laborious flight as you suddenly appear out of the fog far closer than he would normally permit. A watery sun – a bright white circle in a white sky – pierces through the moving vapour, gradually lifting and thinning the mist until it finally departs completely.

Maybe though, you come here in winter when the bare-banked rhynes are thick with ice which, when broken, reveals deep-brown water remarkably clear for all its peat-staining. Hoar-frost clings to everything; ice jewels glisten on the fine boney stems which formerly bore the long-departed white flowers of cow parsley. A gate-post is thickened by a coating of frost and a nearby plank bridge bears the black prints of a fox where warm pads have melted the ice.

Spring brings winds hurtling in from the Atlantic with nothing to impede their passage. Willow trees bend and lash, the river is lifted into waves and white foam collects among the reeds. Rooks and crows take to the wing from the fields and are immediately carried away, while smaller birds cower in the cover of thickets. Rain, and sometimes hail, arrives in sheets bearing down in slanting curtains and stinging hands and face.

A summer walk is a different tale: high above, larks sing noisily or parachute down on half-closed wings. The heavy scent of meadow sweet hangs on the balmy air and yellow irises colour the banks of the rhynes now green and thick with vegetation. Peewits tumble and cry, their crests akimbo and swans swim idly past accompanied by fluffy cygnets.

If driving, park your vehicle at the end of the track being careful not to block any entrance and set off southwards. I have chosen to concentrate on your left of the path throughout because you will be coming back up this path in due course.

The first large tree on the far side of the ditch (rhyne) is an *alder* and is a typical tree of wet ground. Nitrogen is essential to plant growth and in boggy areas, where the soil is waterlogged, this element is scarce. Alder roots form an association with a bacteria which enables them to extract nitrogen from the atmosphere thus permitting the alder to grow in places where other trees cannot. Furthermore, the tree actually puts nitrogen into the surrounding soil. This increased fertility, together with the gradual raising of the ground-level by shed alder leaves, dead branches and, finally, by the trees themselves falling, means that other tree species can move into an area which is both drier and more fertile than before the alder arrived. The section of woodland a little further along the track on the left, which is a mixture of alder and *birch*, demonstrates this.

It is not unusual to see the woody remains of last year's cones, this year's seed-laden fruits and next year's vestigial male catkins all on the same alder branch in autumn.

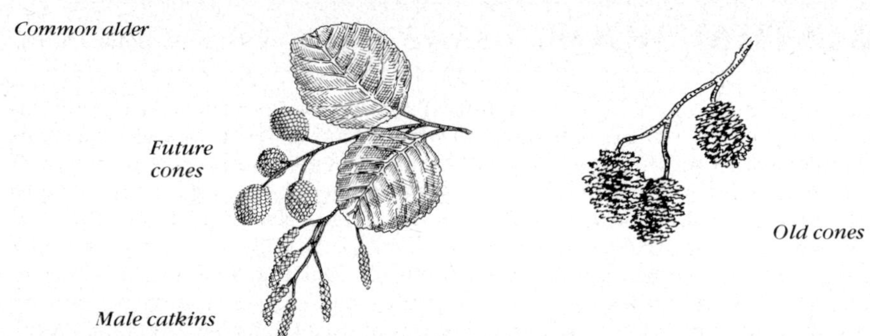

Common alder

In early spring, alders have male catkins and tiny reddish female flowers. Each heavily-veined leaf has a dent at the tip where most similar leaves are pointed and in autumn the little green fruits appear. These are like miniature conifer cones and have led to the alder being called Britain's only broad-leafed conifer. At one time, alder wood was used in the making of clogs but nowadays their major function, from man's point of view, is to hold together the banks of streams and rivers with their roots.

The sides of the track or 'drove' as it is called, are well endowed with a wide variety of flowers. At the gateway into this wood is *burdock* which blooms from June onwards and has thistle-like purple flowers and broad heart-shaped leaves. Already clustered around the flowers are the little hooks which are attached to the seeds. When they are ripe, these cling to any passing object and are thus dispersed to new areas. Children know these burrs well and often throw them at one another in an effort to make them stick to clothing; they may also know burdock from the fact that an essence from the plant is used to make dandelion and burdock pop.

Burdock
Its hooked seeds cling to passing objects

There are also members of the umbellifer family growing alongside the drove. Among them you may find *angelica* with its many white flowers clustered into umbrella-like hemispheres, which like those of its relatives, *cow parsley* and *hog weed*, are then grouped at the head of the stem. They are much loved by insects. *Soldier beetles* – long orange insects with black tips to their wing-cases – are found on them in July and August and can often be seen mating there. In fact, soldier beetles are carnivorous and probably wait on umbellifers, such as angelica, to pounce on unwary insects visiting these attractive flowers. While the flowers are in evidence from July, the plant is easily recognisable before that by its leaves which are similar to those of ash trees, and by the cup-like sheath around each leaf stem where it joins the main stalk. It is from the cultivated form that the candied-green cake decoration is made.

In June, too, you should be able to detect the heavy fragrance of meadow sweet which also likes these damp areas. At first glance it is like angelica, growing to almost the same height, but its flowers are more creamy in less-ordered flowerheads, its stems are red and leaves more defined, having a veined upper surface and a light downy lower one. Its delightful scent led to its being used in medieval times as a floor-covering along with rushes and it is also said to have similar medicinal properties to those of aspirin.

At the end of the woodland along the field-edge is a *birch* tree with large bunches of tiny .branches growing in clumps. These are called witches' brooms and are caused by a virus, fungus or an insect stimulating tiny buds, which would not normally grow at all, into abnormal growth. This freak growth, while looking odd, causes only minor harm to the tree itself.

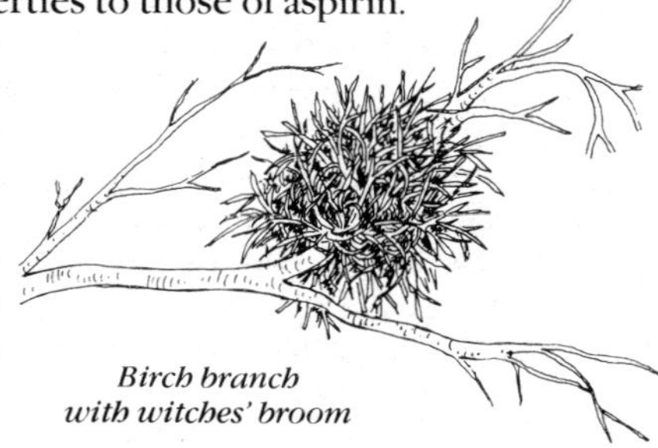

Birch branch with witches' broom

Just before the bridge there is a gateway into which stone has been imported to strengthen the track, as this soft peaty ground is very spongy. You may also see pieces of leather – industrial offcuts from the local shoe industry. In the north of England, in similar situations, old conveyor-belting from the pits is used.

The climb onto the bridge is quite steep. This is because the structure has been lifted well above the North Drain here so as not to impede the water flow in times of flood. Once on the bridge carefully scan the water and the banks. You should see *mute swans* and possibly the still grey form of a *heron* and if you are very lucky, the blue flash of a *kingfisher*. The backs and the wings of these birds are turquoise while their breasts and underparts are a rich almost orange chestnut. They live on fish which they catch either by waiting patiently on a perch above the water or by hovering over the surface. Then they plunge into the water, capture their prey and fly back to their perch.

If a kingfisher catches a spiny fish, i.e. a bullhead or stickleback, it will beat it against its perch until dead and eat it head first lest the fins and spines catch in its throat as the fish is being swallowed.

Kingfisher killing a fish against its perch

Kingfishers nest in a burrow two to three feet long which they excavate themselves in the river bank. The eggs are round and white. Eggs laid in an exposed location, such as a ledge on sea cliff, are usually very pointed so that, if disturbed, they will roll around in a circle and not fall over the edge and smash on the rocks below; those of the kingfisher could hardly be less exposed and so any shaping is superfluous. Furthermore, eggs found in cup-shaped nests or laid on the ground have cryptic coloration, they are camouflaged so as to disguise them from the eyes of predators; if anything, eggs laid at the end of a dark tunnel need to be visible to the parent birds rather than hidden from them to avoid accidental breakages and thus white would be the preferred colour.

When the eggs hatch, the chicks are fed on *minnows*, *sticklebacks* and a few large insects such as dragonflies. The nest chamber is soon knee deep in old fish-bones and other debris to the extent that the parents have to wash when they emerge. The young kingfishers have to learn how to fish when they leave the nest and the adults will continue to feed them until this is accomplished.

This sort of river was once a normal part of an otter's habitat and while the *otter* is almost extinct in England, a few still survive on the Somerset Levels, you would, however, be extremely lucky to see one here. The decline of the otter was first noticed in the early seventies when the Mammal Society looked into the records of otter hunts and discovered a serious drop in the number of 'finds' between 1957 and 1967. Further investigations pointed to the heavy use of some pesticides as being one of the major reasons for this and although these chemicals are now banned, other pressures have come to bear on the already depleted otter population.

Otters
They are now very rare and totally protected

The otter's favourite food seems to be *eels*, with course fish and *frogs* following a close second. This type of prey is easy to catch and abundant in the muddier, slow-moving lowland rivers – the sort of waterways which have become so popular for water sports which create disturbances that otters cannot stand. These same rivers are maintained in a clear state by the various drainage authorities who remove bankside trees and bushes in order to allow access for their machines. The North Drain is a good example of this sort of clearance and of the straight waterways that are so good for drainage but not for otters. Bankside cover is essential both for lying up during the day but, more important still, for breeding. Fortunately some of the more enlightened authorities are clearing the bank on only one side of the river to let their dredgers in, although this action may not be in time to save the otter.

Where it is possible, otters have moved up into the hills and away from the often crowded and polluted bare lowland waters. Here the streams run faster and food is scarcer so the animals tend to be thinner on the ground. The network of sluggish waterways on the Somerset Levels was always considered to be an otter's paradise and while the animal was declining elsewhere in England, it remained in fairly large numbers in this area. Research over the past ten years or so has shown that, sadly, even here the otter population is dwindling and it could be that there are now too few otters on the Levels for them ever to build up their population again.

As you progress down the drove you will leave the open fields and enter an area of peat digging. On the left of the track piles of loose peat are covered with *chickweed* – a lush low-growing plant which has tiny white star flowers even in the depths of winter. It was once eaten as a spring salad and is a great coloniser of disturbed ground.

Chickweed
Once eaten as salad

This whole area through which the drove runs is part of the peat extraction industry for which the Levels are well known. Peat – partially decomposed vegetable matter which has been compacted – was cut into small bricks, dried and used for burning and, to some extent, for gardens. Peat is a slow-burning fuel, which does not give off much heat but is very fragrant.

When demand for these uses was low, peat banks were allowed to regenerate after cutting and new peat would form fairly quickly. Nowadays the demand for peat in gardens is much greater and huge areas of the material are excavated, stacked, bagged and sold in garden centres and the like, without giving the peat a chance to re-make itself.

The effects are far reaching for, in order to excavate the peat efficiently, large machines are used and the water table is lowered by pumping which dries the marshy ground around the peat areas. This, in turn, alters the vegetation depriving water-loving species of moisture and allowing plants preferring drier ground to invade and colonise. Thus, although some parts of the Levels are reserved for conservation purposes because many of the plants and some of the animals and birds are rare here, the pumping activities can even alter these and make them less viable.

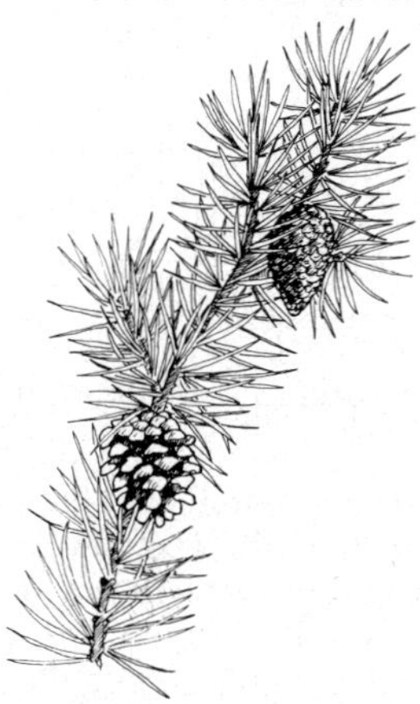

Scots pine branch with cones which open to shed their seeds when ripe

In some places you may also see the straight vertical cut in the soil left by the peat-cutter which slices out blocks much more rapidly than old-fashioned hand cutting and leaves neat pieces to be stacked and dried ready for carting. Looking across the diggings on the left of the drove is a woodland of birch and alder and among them on both sides of the track are tall evergreen trees. These are *scots pines*. Although conifers, they do not grow in the typical 'pyramidal' Christmas-tree shape of most of the others but tend to have a more random arrangement of branches. It is on the upper parts of the trunk that the bark is chestnut in colour, a hue which is especially striking in the low sunlight at dawn or dusk. The blue-green needles grow in pairs and in winter you should be able to spot two different types of cone on the tree, tiny first-year cones on the tips of the branches and larger more-easily-recognisable green two-year-old cones which ripen in spring.

In this area you should find *teasels* – easily identifiable in spring by their prickly stems and backbone of spines that follow the centre of the underside of the leaf. The leaves themselves form a cup around the main stem which collects water and often small insects and which, after a while, begins to smell rather foetid. In July and August the purple flowers appear in a spiny head which always looks flea-bitten and incomplete. When the flowers are finished, the spiny head remains and persists well into winter. It is this seedhead, with its many tiny hooks, that was once used to raise the nap on newly-woven cloth. A sub-species was grown, especially in Somerset, for the sole purpose of 'teasing' cloth in this way. Some people like to grow it in their gardens to attract *goldfinches* which eat the seeds.

Goldfinches are beautiful little birds with red and white face patches and a black cap. On their wings is a yellow flash which becomes a golden wing stripe in flight. The red face feathers are stiff and strong and act as guard feathers against the spines of their foodplants which include *thistles* and burdock as well as non-spiky *groundsel* and *dandelion*. You may see a twittering flock or 'charm' of goldfinches feeding here.

The goldfinches' happy song made it a popular bird to capture and cage during the last century. This is not legal in Britain now but many birds are still caught and caged in other European countries.

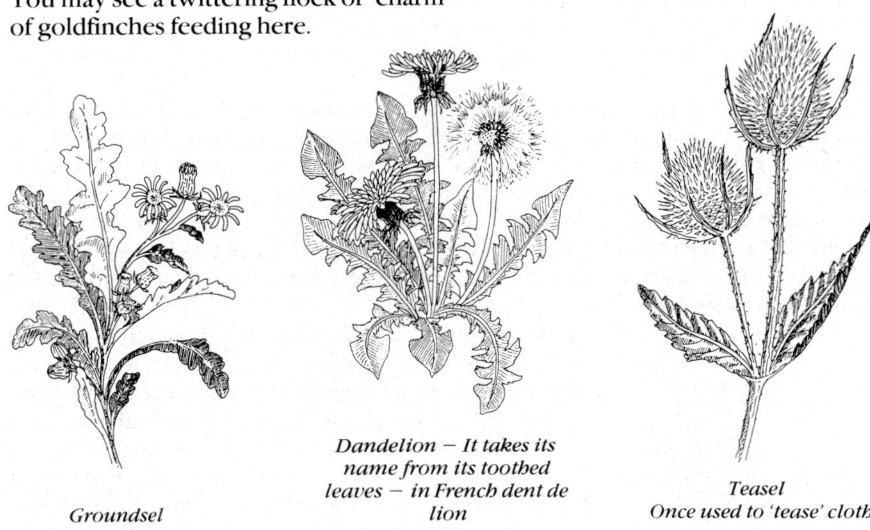

Groundsel

Dandelion – It takes its name from its toothed leaves – in French dent de lion

Teasel
Once used to 'tease' cloth

Turn round at the large oak tree at the corner of the woodland on your right and retrace your steps.

Look out across the diggings in the wetter areas for *greater reedmace* (bulrushes). The most recognisable feature of this plant is its beautiful dark-brown seed-head which is formed in July but does not shed its seeds until the following February. Anyone collecting these for decoration will know to their cost how the windborne seeds suddenly spring from within the brown outer coating in a shower of white fluff.

16 *Pass out of the peat diggings and back into the farmland.*

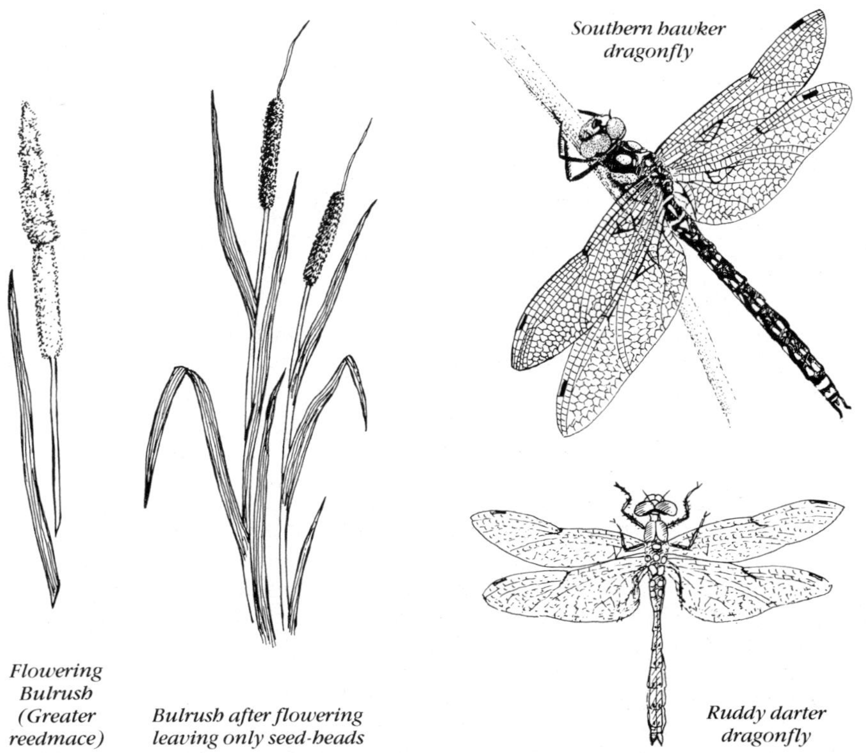

Flowering Bulrush (Greater reedmace)

Bulrush after flowering leaving only seed-heads

Ruddy darter dragonfly

The meadows here are frequently damp and sometimes flood in winter. The spiky groups of rushes among the grass are indicators of wet soil and the deep rhynes on either side of the drove are important to help drain the water from the land. They are also used as 'wet fences' for, being both deep and water-logged, they prevent farm animals from straying. Although they may appear black and glossy in winter, these watercourses teem with life in summer months.

Alongside them may grow *irises* (yellow flags) with their beautiful and brilliant yellow flowers in May and June. Later in the year, the heavy bright-green pointed seed pods appear and are easy to spot. *Moorhens* skulk in the rhyne bottoms and even nest in their undergrowth and often the silent stealthy heron will fish the banks. Dragonflies and damsel flies frequent this area. The dragonfly is the bigger of the two and holds its wings outspread when at rest while the damsel fly holds its wings together down its back. Dragonflies are very helicopter like and their whirring wings make an audible rustle in flight as they hunt up and down these waterways seeking their prey.

The dragonfly you are most likely to see in this area is the *southern hawker* – one of the larger members of this species; you may also notice *ruddy darters* which are stubbier-bodied brilliant-red dragonflies and are less common in Britain. Look, too, for red damsel flies in September in particular, when these insects can frequently be found perching on rocks and gates, possibly in order to obtain the heat that these objects have absorbed from the sun.

In the fields on your left you may spot both *peewits* (lapwings) – those apparently black and white birds with crests – and *curlews*, with the long downcurved bill and mournful cry. If you are quiet, the sheltered drove can conceal your presence to enable you to watch *hares* that are sometimes visible in these fields. Much larger than *rabbits*, hares are the high-speed racers of British mammals and even at slow speeds they will cover three metres in a single bound. While apparently similar, hares are unlike rabbits in almost every way. They live entirely above ground, relying on camouflage or speed to escape from danger. Hares make small nests (forms) in the grass and will sit absolutely still in these until you almost tread on them. They then spring up at great speed, clearing the ground in enormous leaps and jumping hedges and bramble thickets in their efforts to get away. Although, by and large, they live solitary lives, hares are seen together at mating time in spring. The young (leverets) are not born blind and naked like baby rabbits but are fully furred and ready to run. The mother disperses them in a number of individual forms which she visits to allow them to suckle. If one of the leverets is discovered by a predator, the others have a chance of escape.

Peewits (lapwings) in summer. Their apparently black wings are in fact a beautiful dark green

You may have spotted metal objects in some of the fields with stock in, from which a hose-pipe snakes down into the nearby rhyne. These are drinking facilities for the cattle. In attempting to drink they press down on a bar which operates a pump and they draw their own water up from the ditch. This prevents the animals trying to reach the water in the bottom of the rhyne and becoming stuck in the mud or escaping from the field.

Return to your starting point.

Hare
March is a good time to look out for them

Notes

Notes

House martin
Swallows
Rowan
Trig. point
Stonechat
Bracken
Wheatear on gorse
Meadow pipit
Marbled white
Whortleberry
Skylark
Bell heather
Cross leaved heath
Large white

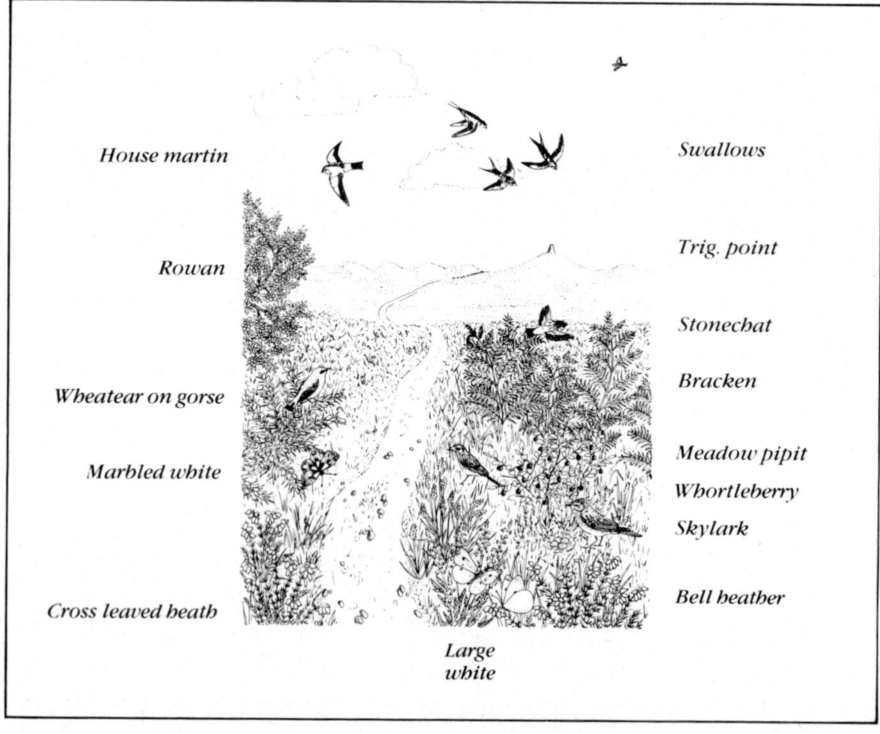

Black Down

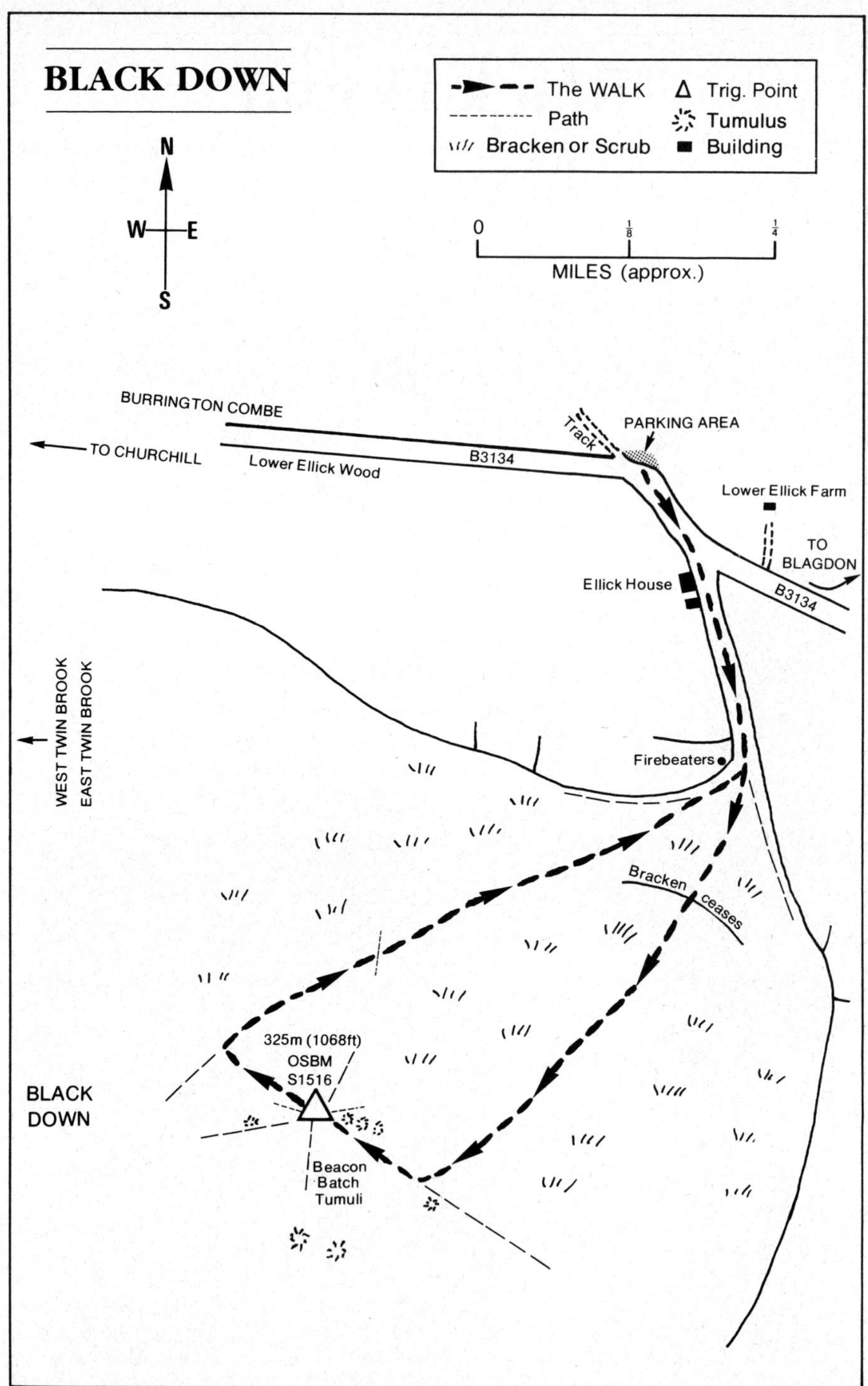
BLACK DOWN
The WALK
Path
Bracken or Scrub
Trig. Point
Tumulus
Building
N
W
E
S
0
1/8
1/4
MILES (approx.)
BURRINGTON COMBE
TO CHURCHILL
Lower Ellick Wood
B3134
Track
PARKING AREA
Lower Ellick Farm
TO BLAGDON
Ellick House
B3134
WEST TWIN BROOK
EAST TWIN BROOK
Firebeaters
Bracken ceases
325m (1068ft)
OSBM
S1516
BLACK DOWN
Beacon Batch Tumuli

BLACK DOWN

O.S. ST45(490580) – Hilly walk

Climb to the highest spot on Mendip and look for miles over rolling hills and silvery sea. Black Down's acid moorland can be wet and will act like a sponge if it has rained recently so wellies may be advisable. High points are often windy so wrap up well if it is cold or wet for this hilly walk of almost two miles.

At the top of Burrington Combe on the left is a large parking area and almost opposite, on the right and higher up on the hill, is a lay-by with a track leading off it past Ellick House. Follow this track with the house and its red post-box on your right and walk up into the hills.

Here and there the surface of the track itself is hard grey limestone, the very bones of the hill which have been swept clean by running water and passing feet. It is smooth and water-worn as the rain, which collects carbon dioxide in falling, is sufficiently acid to dissolve the rock.

Beside the track are *blackthorn* bushes. These are unmistakable for, as their name suggests, they have black bark and thorns often very long and sharp which, if you are unlucky enough to be pierced by one, seem to leave an irritant inside your skin to cause soreness for some time after your encounter. Their fine creamy-white flowers can be seen in early April and, in cold springs, arrive before the leaves appear giving a beautiful contrast of a dark bush with white blossom. The fruit in autumn is well known to makers of sloe gin for the blackthorn is the source of the sloe fruit. Sloes are dark blue in colour, with a white bloom, and taste extremely bitter. The initial nibble is not nasty but suddenly the berry seems actually to dry up the mouth.

The trees growing on either side are *ash* and can be identified by their light-grey bark, especially on the branches, and in winter by their dark-grey buds. The leaves are compound and have a single stalk with individual saw-edged leaves growing in opposite pairs along its length. The flowers consist of frothy bunches of stems terminating in purple-brown tips which grow in clumps from its twigs before the leaves appear on the tree. Indeed ash, like oak, is almost the last tree to come into leaf and features in an old country rhyme which supposedly foretells the coming summer's rainfall:

If oak comes out before the ash
We will only have a splash.
If ash comes out before the oak
We will surely have a soak!

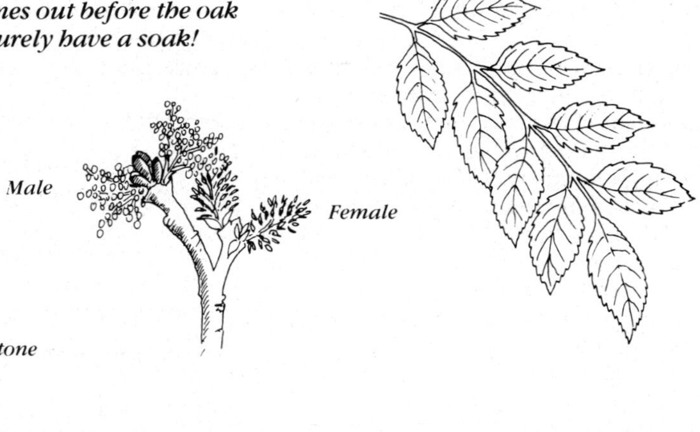

Ash flowers and leaves. The ash is a good indicator of limestone

Ash fruits are called keys and are winged seeds which form in bunches and spiral away on the breeze when ripe. Ash is a very typical tree of limestone country as it likes alkaline or base rich soils. It is common on Mendip, especially in Burrington Combe and the Cheddar and Ebbor Gorges and in other limestone areas such as parts of the Peak District National Park.

You may see 'white' butterflies on this limestone grassland although not all will belong to the 'white' family for some, strangely enough, will probably be members of the 'browns'. *Large whites* are often here. They are creamy-white butterflies with black tips to the leading edges of the forewings and are the *cabbage white* of gardens. Here though they will choose wild members of the cabbage family such as *bedge mustard* on which to lay their eggs.

The *marbled white*, which is about the same size as the large white but with pretty dappled-white markings, is in fact a 'brown'. Its larvae (caterpillars) feed on grass and the female lays her eggs in a most haphazard fashion: she merely scatters them among the grass stems as she flies.

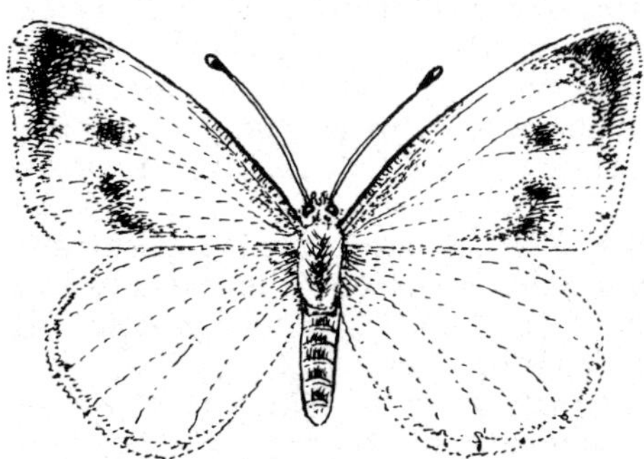

Large cabbage white (female) – A member of the 'white' family

Marbled white (male) – A member of the 'brown' family

At the top of the track where it comes out onto the hillside, the main route bears round to the right past a set of firebeaters while you go straight on up the narrower path.

The presence of the firebeaters is particularly significant at this point for the whole of this northern hillside in front is dominated by a sheet of *bracken*. You may spot this ubiquitous fern in spring, unfurling its fronds from among last year's stems. If it comes out too early, frost will brown the soft new ends to the leaves. A little later on you will see the landscape before you covered in a delightful light-green carpet; this will gradually darken as the year progresses and the plant grows taller; consequently, by high summer, the bracken will be above the shoulders of all but the tallest. In autumn bracken browns and dies back taking on a gingery-golden hue in low afternoon sunlight like the coat of an orang-utan. See illustration of bracken on page 110.

Parts of the bracken are razor sharp and will cause fine deep cuts in unprotected hands and legs – so resist temptation to pull at the leaves or stems or even to run through it.

MENDIP PROFILE

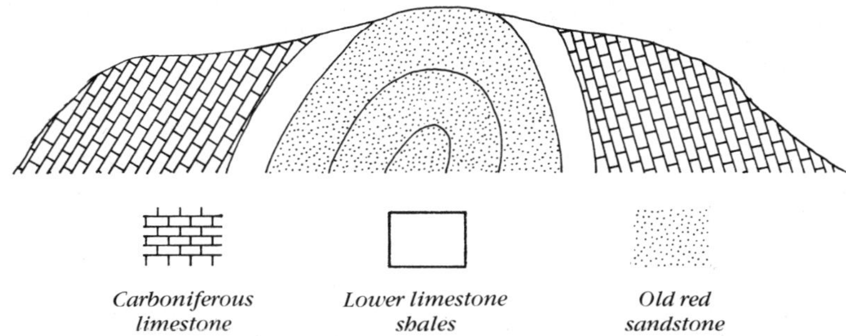

At one time, in areas where few cereals were grown and straw was scarce, bracken was used for animal bedding even though, if eaten in quantity by stock, it is poisonous. Now, with improved transport systems to move straw from cereal areas and land improvement enabling more farmers to grow corn, this is no longer necessary. The bracken here owes its existence to frequent fires which sweep up from Burrington Combe from time to time – hence the firebeaters. Its underground rhizomes protect it from the flames and allow the plant to rise Phoenix-like from the ashes when all else is destroyed.

At about the point that you leave the bracken, the underlying rock changes from limestone to sandstone. The ground will start to feel different underfoot. The rock itself is gritty and, as its names implies, like many tiny gravel grains all stuck together making it rough and coarse to the touch. Sandstone is impervious (water will not drain through it) and it does not crack and fissure as limestone does. The soil on the sandstone here is peaty as the vegetation is not broken down to the same extent as on limestone, because of the lack of oxygen in these water-logged conditions.

You are walking up to the highest point on Mendip and it is ironical that the highest point of a range of hills well known for being limestone, is in fact formed from sandstone. The truth of the matter is that the softer limestone has been dissolved and eroded away from the top of the fold or anticline to reveal the more hardwearing old red sandstone beneath. The sandstone outcrops at only three other places on Mendip, all of them high points. They are North Hill at Priddy, Beacon Hill close to Shepton Mallet and Pen Hill near Wells on which stands the very tall TV mast.

If it is not a time of drought, the path will be wetter than on the limestone and the plant-life changes quite suddenly. For the skilled botanist, this change is enormous but even the untrained eye can spot some changes. The bracken ceases and this in itself is odd for the plant normally shuns limestone soils and seeks acid ones. As we have seen, fire has enabled bracken to spread on the limestone and the same fire has been extinguished by the wet nature of the acid sandstone soil thus preventing further spread of the bracken. It is replaced by low-growing woody plants like *whortleberry*, *heather*, *gorse* and *purple moor grass*.

Whortleberry (blaeberry, bilberry). Very tasty in pies

Whortleberry has a number of other names including bilberry and blaeberry and its fruit is much favoured by Americans. The leaves and stems of this plant turn a beautiful red in autumn but by then the small sweet black berries, which are ripe in July, will probably have already disappeared.

There are three types of heather here: *bell heather* and *common heather* (ling) – the former having bigger and redder flowers – and *cross leaved heath* which can be identified by the arrangement of its leaves around the stem in whorls of four.

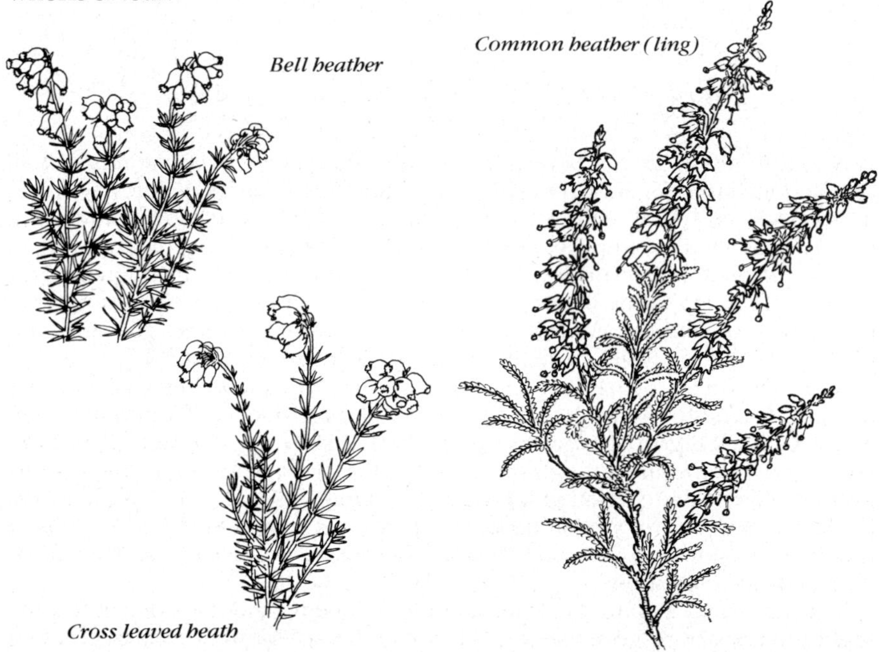

Look back near the top of the slope for, on a clear day, you can see the sparkling waters of Blagdon and Chew Valley lakes and in the distance the sea with the Black Mountains and the Brecon Beacons on the far side of the Channel.

At the strong wide cross track, turn right towards the trig. point.

In summer especially, there should be a variety of birds here; listen first for *skylarks* singing high in the sky. You may just be able to spot one hovering against the brightness or see a lark parachute down on half-closed wings to land in the grass and disappear from view. A speckle-breasted *meadow pipit* may be making its high-voiced call from vegetation around about, and perhaps too you will hear the sound of someone knocking two pebbles together. This is really the contact call of the *stonechat* – a bird a little smaller than a robin. The male stonechat has a black head, white collar and chestnut breast. Look out too for a very smart bird on the path or a nearby mound. As you draw near, it will fly off a little way showing a white patch on the converts above its tail and revealing itself as a *wheatear*. Unlike the previous three birds, this is a summer migrant, wintering in warmer climates and only coming to Britain to breed before leaving again in autumn.

Wheatears – One of the earlier summer migrants to arrive

Stonechats – Their call is like the clacking together of stones

You will probably have noticed that there is no shortage of mounds for wheatears to use. Some of them, the round ones, are Bronze Age tumuli and make up a collection called Beacon Batch. These round barrows (burial mounds) are remnants of the early Bronze Age dating from 1700 to 1200 BC, and other groups are to be found on North Hill and Beacon Hill, both high points mentioned already.

Not to be confused with the round barrows are a large number of other mounds dating back only as far as World War II. They were constructed here as a decoy town to attract enemy bombers.

Make your way to the triangulation point OSBM S1516.

This concrete marker stands at 1,068 feet which, it may be considered, makes Black Down a mountain if you take 1,000 feet as when hills end and mountains begin. Although it can be very cold and bleak here in bad weather, it is hardly worthy of the name, especially when surrounded by the lush emerald-green fields of grass growing on limestone.

As a high point the views are superb on a clear day. From Pen Hill, with its extremely tall mast to the south-east, turn southwards to note the silver shapes of farm buildings in the middle-ground and the rocks of Cheddar Gorge beyond. In the distance, past the Poldens – a hogsback ridge of hills which runs from Street to Bridgwater – the Quantocks can be seen and, if it is really clear, Exmoor too. On the far side of Bridgwater Bay, standing on Somerset's north coast, are the large concrete boxes of Hinkley Point nuclear power station.

Down in the valley, the rim of Cheddar reservoir should be visible. To the north of the reservoir the top of the bare rockface of Callow Quarry is just visible which stands at the end of the long straight track. To the right of this are the trees of Rowberrow Warren.

Rowberrow Warren is a plantation of mostly conifers although there is a proportion of *beech* trees for amenity and firebreak purposes. The conifer species are *sitka* and *Norway spruce*, the latter being the traditional Christmas tree, *Scots* and *Corsican pine* and *larch*. Sitka spruce and Corsican pine are particularly planted because of their rapid growth and the former, which hails from Alaska, produces more timber in a shorter time than any other tree. Except for the beech, all the above species are softwoods and have been introduced into Britain for commercial purposes.

Although it appears dense from a distance, the plantation is thinned from time to time to remove smaller trees which are used for fencing or pulp thus allowing the best specimens to grow more freely.

Almost due west above the plantation is Brean Down with Steep Holm and Flat Holm (with its lighthouse) situated beyond that. Turning north past Weston-super-Mare there is a further area of woodland – beyond Wrington – and the swathe cut by a pylon line is clearly visible passing over the skyline.

Walk away from the trig. point, with the numbers side at your back, along the more defined of the two paths. At the major path that crosses at right angles, turn right.

Look on your left here for the start of a small stream valley – the easternmost course of a pair of streams known as East Twin Brook and West Twin Brook. They run down to a whole series of medium-sized caves for which the Burrington area is famous. East Twin terminates at East Twin Swallet or Swallow Hole – so called because the earth appears to swallow the water. Swallets are apparent in many parts of Mendip. Some are like funnels with caves leading on from the

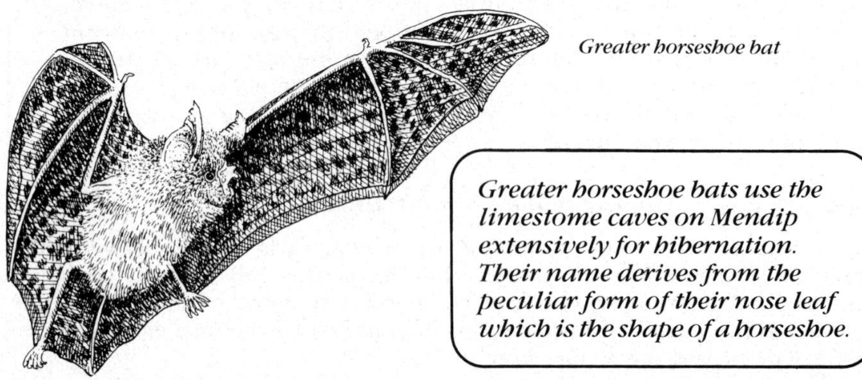

Greater horseshoe bat

Greater horseshoe bats use the limestome caves on Mendip extensively for hibernation. Their name derives from the peculiar form of their nose leaf which is the shape of a horseshoe.

bottom of the deep depression like that of Rod's Pot, while in others the cave entrance is choked and water simply filters through the rocks into underground passages. Choked swallets are sometimes excavated by enthusiastic pot-holers intent on discovering new caves like that of Sidcot Swallet which was 'dug' by members of the Sidcot School Speleological Society in 1925. On other occasions, usually after prolonged heavy rain or storms, the choke is cleared by the pressure of water and a new cave reveals itself to the eager explorer. One such is Grebe Swallet in Velvet Bottom which was first opened up by the flood of July 1968.

In the drier and sunnier areas of the hillside you may come across *adders* (vipers). One of the two common snakes in Britain, adders prefer to inhabit dry heathland areas where they can bask in the sun and hunt the small mammals upon which they prey. The nature of their food means that the snake has to be poisonous, for it would be very difficult to capture and kill lively prey such as shrews and mice without this weapon. The snake stalks its quarry, bites it, injecting its venom, and then withdraws to avoid being bitten itself until the animal succumbs, it then swallows its meal whole, relying upon its powerful digestive juices to break down its prey.

More people have died from insect stings in the last 85 years than from adder bites.

Adders are easy to recognise, for, although their base colour may vary from light green to dark green through to an almost chestnut red, they have a distinctive and heavily-marked dark zigzag line along their back to their neck, and on the back of the head is a 'V' mark or an inverted 'A' from which they are said to take their name. They are shorter and stockier than *grass snakes* and tend to avoid water which the grass snake enjoys. The pupils of their eyes are slit vertically to form a diamond shape unlike the round eye of the grass snake.

Adders are viviparous (i.e. they produce live young as opposed to the grass snake which lays eggs) and do not have to rely on the heat of the sun for incubation, thus enabling them to spread further north, as far as the top of Scotland in fact.

Whilst adders are poisonous, they frighten easily and will hurry away if disturbed. People who get bitten have almost always interfered with the snake in some way and it will have bitten in self-defence. It is much better to leave the reptile alone to depart of its own accord for it will certainly not go out of its way to bite you.

Adder (viper) – Although poisonous, it is harmless if left alone

In summer months there may be *house martins* and *swallows* hawking for insects over the bracken. House martins are stubbier than swallows with a similar but much shorter forked tail. In flight their distinctive white rump and white underparts show up against their black wings and apparently black bodies – their heads and backs are actually dark blue. The upperparts of the swallow are more noticeable dark blue, whilst their underparts are quite pink and their chins and foreheads a reddish chestnut. Both species are members of the same family – eating insects which they catch in flight and living in close association with man. Their mud nests are, in the case of martins, hung under the eaves, while those of swallows may stand on a beam or ledge in an outbuilding or garage. Swallows and martins arrive from Africa in spring and return there in autumn, gathering on telegraph wires beforehand in noisy groups, almost as if discussing their travel plans.

The farm in the valley below, near Ellick House, keeps a herd of Guernsey cows – quite a rarity in a dairy county with a heavy majority of black and white Friesian herds. These cows, which give creamier milk than Friesians, are brown with white bellies and often have white patches on their legs. You will probably see quite a few in the fields nearby.

On the left of the path, here, is a single tree, the highest on the hill. It is a *rowan* (mountain ash) and has leaves remarkably like those of ash even though they do not belong to the same family. The rowan, which does well in acid soils, has white blossoms about May which precede the scarlet berries of early September. Too sour for man's palate, they seem highly desirable to birds and quickly disappear in early autumn. In Scotland the tree has particular significance for crofters and was planted close to the house to protect the holding against witchcraft.

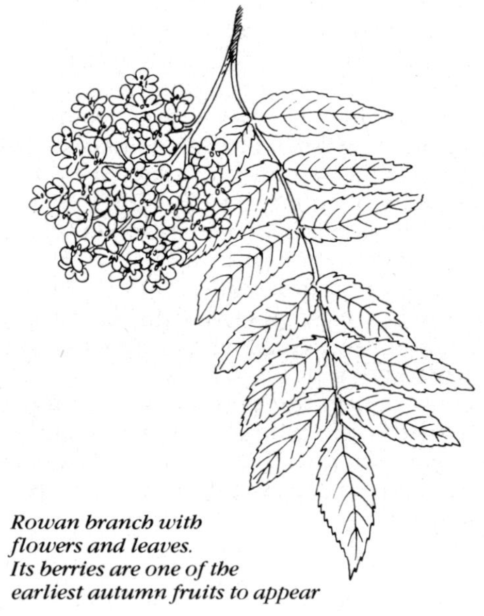

Rowan branch with flowers and leaves. Its berries are one of the earliest autumn fruits to appear

As you descend the hill, you will regain the limestone and then join up with a path near the hedge bordering agricultural land. Follow this with the hedge on your left until you reach the firebeaters. Turn left here and follow the track back down the hill to the road.

Notes

Notes

Cuckoo
Chiff-chaff
Ash
Tufted ducks
Reed warbler on common reed
Holly
Coot
Little owl
Rosebay willowherb
Cow parsley
Peacock
Red admiral
Red campion
Bank vole
Small tortoiseshell on white deadnettle
Thrush
Primrose

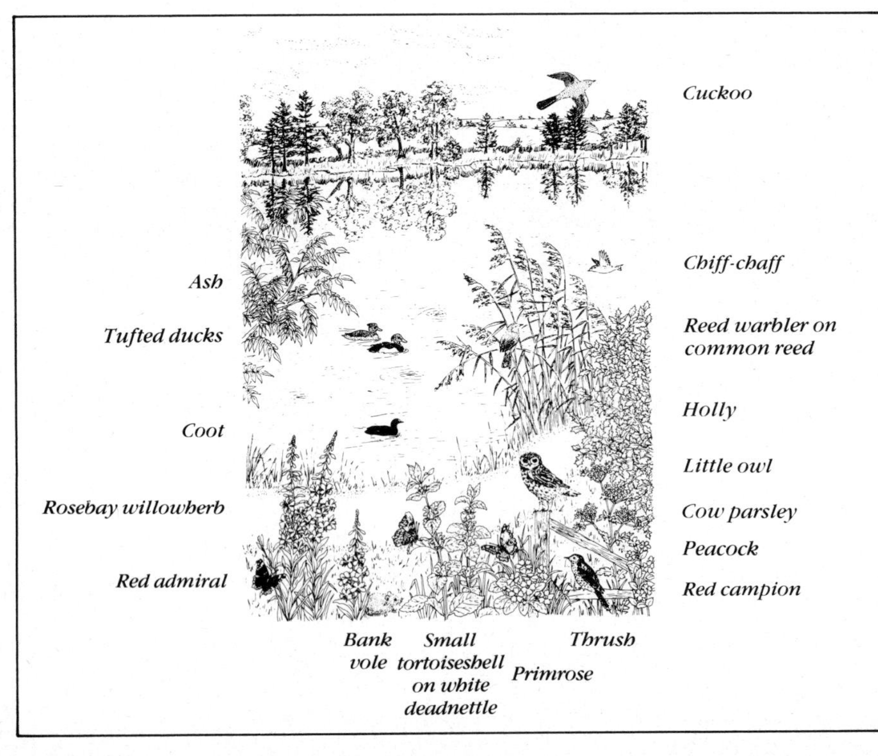

Litton

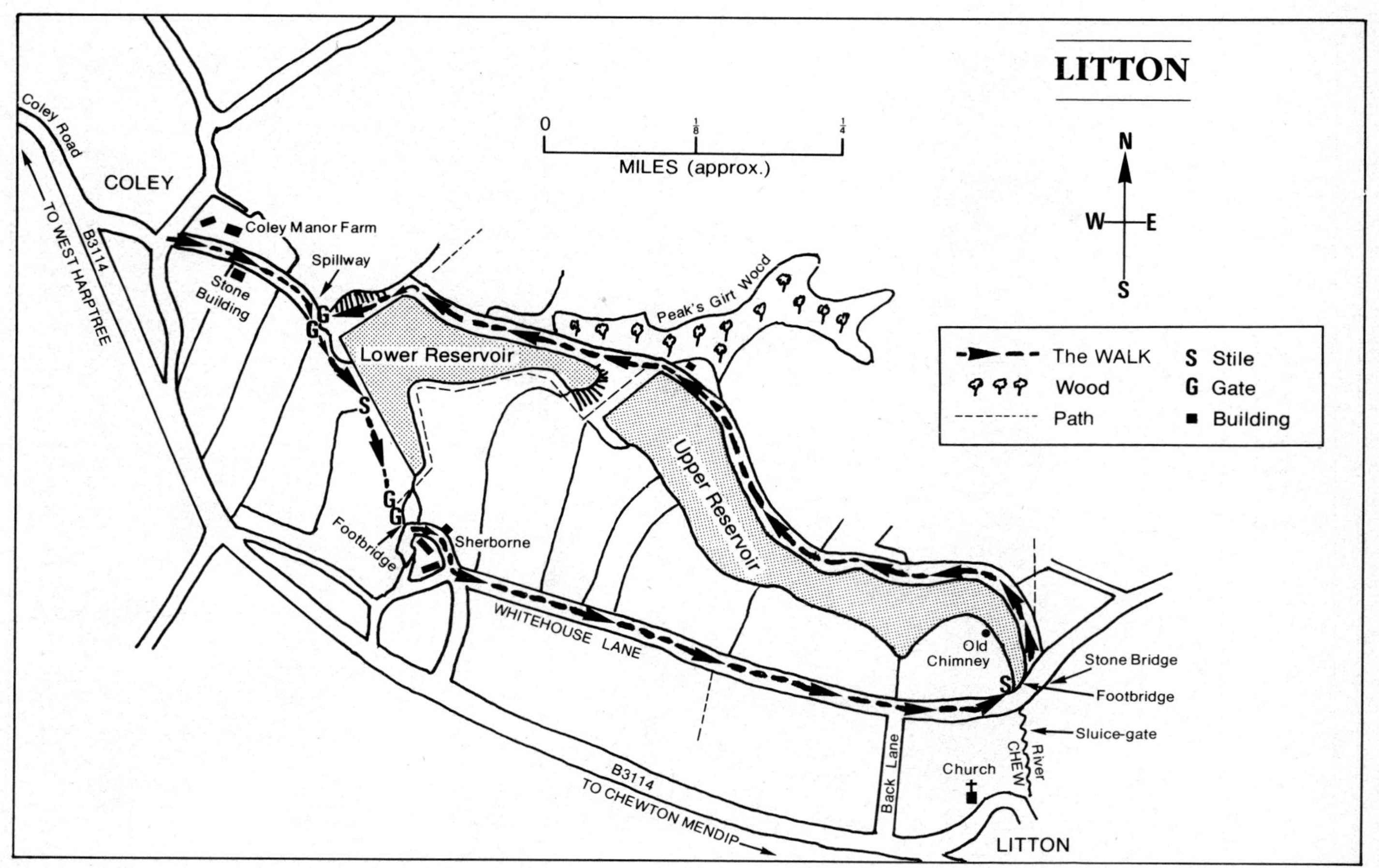
LITTON
0
1/8
1/4
MILES (approx.)
N
W
E
S
The WALK
Wood
Path
S Stile
G Gate
Building
Coley Road
COLEY
TO WEST HARPTREE
B3114
Coley Manor Farm
Spillway
Stone Building
Lower Reservoir
Peak's Girt Wood
Upper Reservoir
Footbridge
Sherborne
WHITEHOUSE LANE
Old Chimney
Stone Bridge
Footbridge
Sluice-gate
River CHEW
Church
Back Lane
B3114
TO CHEWTON MENDIP
LITTON

LITTON

O.S. ST55(583557) – Around two fresh water lakes

The two Litton reservoirs are lakes hidden by folds in the Mendip hills and form the centrepiece of this walk of almost two miles. They straddle the Avon/ Somerset border and, though you start in Somerset, you will walk into Avon and then back into Somerset once more. The route is fairly flat and dry in all but the wettest weather and it's fairly sheltered too. The trees and birds certainly make the journey worthwhile.

The walk starts in the hamlet of Coley and takes you up the access track to the reservoirs. Pass a farm on your left and a large stone building on your right and continue towards the cattle-grid where you turn right, climb the rail fence to the left of the leftmost of the two metal gates and follow the fence around to the left alongside the spillway.

In the right-hand edge of the field is a large, old, pollarded *ash* – the centre of which appears to be completely hollow. Before the hollow area becomes so large, such trees are used extensively by various species of bird. The first may be a species of woodpecker which actually creates the entrance and clears out a chamber inside for its nest or possibly a *starling* which makes use of an existing weakness left by a broken branch. An increase in the hole size could allow owls to enter and rear their broods, and both *little owls* and *tawny owls* will use such locations. It is quite likely, though, that the site will eventually become uninhabitable as the tree continues to rot down to the base. Large mammals will then take over. I have found *fox* dens (earths), with one or two additional underground entrances, centred on such a hollow tree. *Badgers* may sometimes use them as 'day nests' which are lying-up places located away from the main

Vixen with cubs – Foxes are often easier to see in towns than in the country

sett in hidden sites. The badger will bring in large quantities of dry grass and leaves and use the nest either for lying up during the day or, more commonly, for resting part-way through the night. Having eaten a good meal of earthworms – its favourite food – the badger will, rather than return to the sett, often have an after-dinner nap in such a day nest.

The reservoirs here have recently been refurbished and the area between the fence and the spillway has been planted with shrubs. You will see *holly* here, amongst other species, in black-wire guards to prevent them being damaged by *rabbits* for, when the weather is cold and food is difficult to find, these mammals will eat the bark from small trees and often kill them as a result. The rabbit's mouth is specially designed to do this as it has a split upper-lip which enables the animal to get its teeth close to the trunk and remove the bark efficiently without damage to itself. Ultimately the rabbit has the edge on the forester as, in very cold weather when there is deep snow, the raised ground level enables it to reach above the rabbit-guard and remove the bark higher up the tree or even the leading shoot from the top of the stem!

The rabbit's front incisors grow continually to make up for hard wear. If fed only soft food and with nothing hard to chew, its teeth would continue to grow, eventually curling round and becoming useless, causing the rabbit to die of starvation.

Cross the double stile.

The hedge on the left contains a wide variety of shrubby species and this is indicative of its age. *Field maple* is here – an often neglected tree. Its leaves are five-lobed like the leaf on the Canadian emblem and, in autumn, they turn to a magnificent gold. The fruits are winged, like those of *sycamore*, but joined in pairs horizontally unlike the sycamore's 'V' shape. The field maple is a lover of chalk and limestone but tends to do better in the south-east rather than here where it rarely attains more than shrub size. In Kent, for example, there are records of field maples reaching almost 80 feet.

Hawthorn (quickthorn) is easy to spot in that it has shortish straight thorns. Its leaves sprout fairly early in spring and for a week or so roadside hawthorn hedges look beautiful with just a haze of light-green. Once they emerge fully, the leaves are three- or five-lobed and are followed in May by masses of scented white blossom – hence may-blossom. The dull round red fruits (haws) stand out in autumn once the leaves have fallen giving the small hawthorn trees and hedges a reddish appearance. They are much favoured by small birds, particularly members of the thrush family – such as the winter-migrants *fieldfare* and *redwing* – and enjoyed, too, by small mammals which climb the trees to harvest them. Strangely enough, *bank voles* enjoy the flesh and discard the stones whilst *woodmice* throw away the fruit to reach the pip.

Look out for the red twigs and oval pointed leaves of *dogwood*. This species also has white flowers in the spring and black berries in autumn. As it thrives on chalk and limestone ground, the dogwood presents a problem to conservationists by invading downland. If there are no sheep or rabbits present to keep it in check, the shrub will rapidly take over, suckering vigorously.

On the left on the other side of the hedge is an arm of the reservoir containing three plants which remain in their skeletal form well into winter. In the wetter, marshy areas are *reeds*; the tallest grass found in Britain, and grown specifically in East Anglia for thatching. A large bed of reeds looks delightful on a breezy day as the wind ripples through the tall stems in waves, causing them to ebb and flow in a variety of buffs, beiges and browns. They provide nesting places for the *reed warbler* – a bird with buff underparts, a light-brown back, and a rather repetitive song.

The reed warbler is a victim of the parasitic cuckoo. It lays an egg in its hosts' nest and removes one of the eggs relying on the newly-batched cuckoo to tip out the remainder and leaving the parent warblers to rear their large foster fledgling.

Reed warbler

Rosebay willowherb grows here too; a tall plant which, *en masse* in summer, makes a brilliant-purple splash of colour. It has a tall cluster of four-petalled flowers giving way to seeds on cottony plumes which are spread generously on a windy day. Once rare, it began to spread in the middle of the last century possibly as a result of the railway boom, for it is a coloniser of recently-burned ground and is common on railway embankments which are frequently fired to curtail the vegetation. It did well during World War II and rapidly moved into bomb-sites in London and other cities so that, nowadays, it can be found almost anywhere in Britain.

Thirdly, there is a nettlebed here. The green-flowered *stinging nettle*, which is familiar to just about everyone, is the food plant of the caterpillars of the *vanessid* group of butterflies which includes such beautiful insects as the *small tortoiseshell*, the *peacock* and the *red admiral*.

Small tortoiseshells on red valerian

Peacock – It has eyes on its wings like those on the bird

Red admiral

Walk through the wicket gate, turn left through the vertical-barred gate, cross the footbridge and climb the rise between the two houses. Look out for the Scots pine on your left and the beech hedge atop the wall on your right. Turn left at the top into Whitehouse Lane just past the no-through-road sign on your left.

Almost opposite the sign, beside the field entrance, is a double step which has been constructed for horses to jump down. Called a quarry jump, it is a type of obstacle found on cross-country courses such as those held at Badminton, Gloucestershire each year.

This is a typical English country lane, running between hedgerows and with fields on either side. Keep a look out for the runways of foxes and badgers through the hedges. These are rarely opposite one another across the road but tend to be slightly offset. If there is mud, you may see the dainty four-toed track of the fox – its front claws almost touching and a distinct cross visible between the pads – or the broad, flat-footed, five-toed badger track (see pages 114–115 for illustrations of animal tracks). There may be hair too, caught on barbed wire or thorns. Badger hairs are black in the middle with white tips and are coarse while those of the fox are brown or ginger and much finer (see page 112).

There is quite a lot of holly to be found in the hedge on the left. It has small white flowers in May but as the trees are either male or female, only the latter has the well-known, bright-red berries, although these are not produced every year. The dark-green waxy leaves are able to survive even frosty weather and can stay on the plant for up to four years. Generally they are only spiky low down on the tree where they are in danger of being browsed. Higher up, the leaves have no spikes and it is said that they were collected to feed stock, notably in the north.

Many hedgerow flowers can be seen along this lane and you should find *white deadnettle*, with its soft, green leaves without a sting, *red campion* and *cow parsley*. The latter is one of the earliest flowering members of the *umbellifer* family whose prolific white blooms give rise to its country name of 'Queen Anne's lace'. On the verge opposite the turning on the right, three *horse-chestnut* trees have been planted and their hoof-printed leaf scars are easy to see. Crossing the stream on the left is the branch of an ash tree bearing *polypody* ferns. These are fond of moist places and enjoy life in the warm, wet south-west, shunning the east of Britain entirely. See illustration on page 110.

Here, on your right, you can see Litton Church tower and the village itself is no distance away. The river Chew has been penned upstream and tumbles noisily over the sluice-gates. To find a stream like this on Mendip is unusual for most water quickly finds its way underground seeping through cracks in the limestone to create caves and reappearing as resurgences at places like Wookey Hole and Cheddar. It is no wonder that full use was made of the running water in years gone by.

Just before the stone road-bridge, cross the stile on your left, cross the footbridge and follow the path around the side of the reservoir.

This is the Upper Litton Reservoir which was constructed in 1850, four years after the completion of the Lower one. They were both built as compensation reservoirs so that, when Bristol Waterworks Company took its supplies from the spring at Chewton Mendip, those living downstream would not be deprived of water. The river now runs on into Chew Valley Lake.

On the opposite bank, an interesting collection of trees are reflected when the water is still. There are *oaks* – gaunt skeletons with elbows in winter; *larches* – the only deciduous conifer, ash; and *spruce* – which keep their leaves throughout the year. The larch is a beautiful tree with its crooked tops. In spring its needles appear in a delicate shade of green which looks outstanding when set against a background of dark-foliaged spruce trees. At this time, too, it has small pink flowers. The needles turn a rusty-gold in autumn and fall to cover the whole floor of a larch plantation with the same rich colour.

Beside them are the remains of an ivy-clad chimney with a square stone base and brick thereafter. It probably marks the site of one of several mills, used for agricultural purposes, which were located alongside the fast-flowing river Chew before the reservoir was constructed.

Just past the second stile on the right of the path you'll find a *spindle* tree. This species of tree often goes unnoticed, growing no taller than fifteen feet. It has green flowers in spring but comes into its full glory in autumn when it produces shocking-pink fruit capsules, divided into four lobes which split to reveal the orange flesh inside, covering a yellow seed. The fruit is as delightful for its shape – resembling a miniature lantern – as for its colour. The tree takes its name from the use of its wood in the making of hand-spindles for wool-spinning in times past. The hard, white splinter-free wood has ideal properties for such a use.

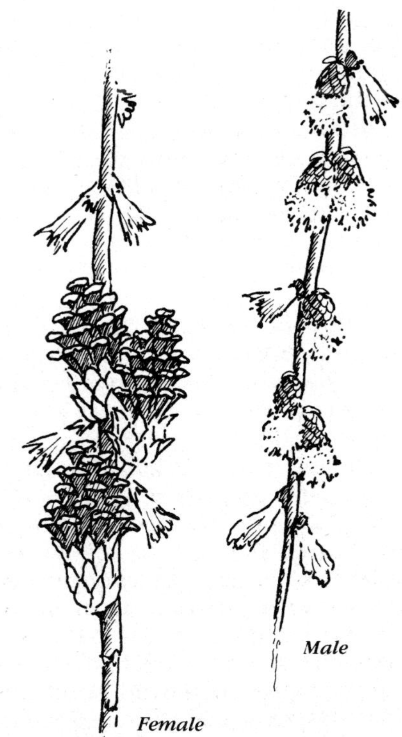

Larch flowers

Dutch elm disease killed about 600,000 trees between 1968 and 1971 of the 18 million elms in southern England.

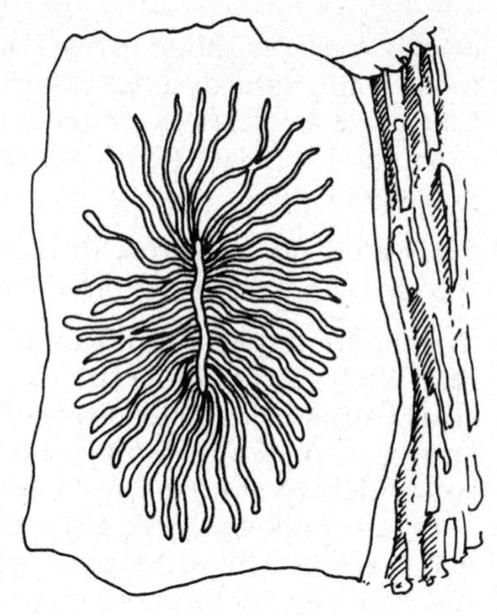

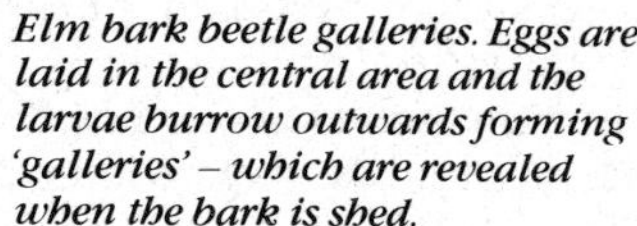

Elm bark beetle galleries. Eggs are laid in the central area and the larvae burrow outwards forming 'galleries' – which are revealed when the bark is shed.

A little further along, on the left-hand side, are some young *elms* whose leaves are rough to the touch. Notice, too, that the two sides of the leaf do not meet in the same place on the stalk. Dutch elm disease killed many mature trees in this area and you will pass one shortly on the right. In many places young elms are thriving and they continue to grow until they give up the sappy skin of youth and take on the proper bark of the adult elm. At this point the *ambrosia beetle* can make its galleries under the bark (you should be able to see these on one of the trees here) and brings with it a fungus which, in turn, kills the layer of wood immediately beneath the bark which contains the veins to carry food throughout the tree. Once this wood is destroyed, the whole tree dies.

Listen out for warblers here during the summer months as two species in particular should be easy to identify by their song. The first is the *chiff-chaff* – which looks remarkably like the willow warbler and even has similarities to the reed warbler. Its song is a giveaway though, for it repeats 'chiff-chaff, chiff-chaff, chiff-chaff' almost all the time. At close quarters you may also catch it making a quiet churring sound to itself. The *willow warbler* arrives a month later, in mid-April, having flown over 2,000 miles from tropical Africa. Its song is a melodic cadence which descends the scale and fades away. Strangely enough, while the chiff-chaff rears only one brood, the busy willow warbler with a month less for the task, manages to bring off two.

As you come past the house, look back across the garden where a tall dark blue-green tree stands. This is an evergreen *holm oak* which has dense foliage to which new leaves are added in June. The acorn cup forms up the side of the acorn so that up to three-quarters of the seed is enclosed.

You have now reached the dam for the top reservoir and there are, on the downstream side, special hollow concrete blocks designed to provide a hard surface which disappear among the grass, making it possible to mow over them. This type of block was designed in the late sixties for temporary car parking and infrequently-used accesses in the countryside so that the general grass cover is maintained and not ruined by vehicle tracks in the soil.

At the bottom of the hill, beside the top of the lower reservoir is an oak tree which has been neatly trimmed and treated to prevent fungal attack. Opposite it you will find a member of the fir family. Many firs are readily identified by the fruity smell the needles emit when they are crushed. An import from North America, firs flower in spring and produce seed-bearing cones in autumn.

A section of water immediately below the upper dam has been cordoned off with a net. This area is used for fish-rearing by the Bristol Waterworks Company's fishery section. A number of water birds collect on both this and the upper reservoir. The most common species you are likely to see is the *coot*. This is a black bird with a white bill and a white forehead or frontal shield. It lives in large flocks in winter but tends to be very territorial and quarrelsome for the rest of the year. It does not have webbed-feet but lobes alongside each of its toes which broaden them to help it swim.

Coots have some difficulty in taking off and have to patter along the surface of the water in order to become airborne. This limits the size of pond they can inhabit.

Although they are sometimes found on the same water, the related *moorhen* takes up residence on smaller ponds shunned by the coot. By contrast, the black moorhen has a red bill and frontal shield, and a white flash on its upright tail which jerks as it swims. This bird is more retiring than the coot, diving out of sight and into cover provided by overhanging vegetation. Both have nests which may be made in conspicuous places and are often raided by predators. Young coots are black and fluffy with ginger heads and, on leaving the nest, they only become independent after about eight weeks.

The moorhen has a white flash on its upright tail and a red frontal shield

The coot has a white frontal shield and no apparent tail

Apart from *mallard*, the other species of duck you should see in any numbers is the *tufted duck*. The drake is black with a white side-flash at the water-line and an almost dark-blue beak. He has a crest on his head from which the bird takes its name. The female is dark brown with a smaller crest. Unlike the mallard, which is a dabbling duck, the tufty is a freshwater diving duck living almost exclusively on small animal life which it hunts during its dives. When it bobs to the surface the oil from the preen gland, with which its feathers are liberally coated, drives off the water like silver beads of mercury, thus preventing the duck from becoming waterlogged and either drowning or dying of cold.

Tufted duck – male

Walk across the dam and pass through the wicket gate to the left of the cattle-grid and return to your starting point.

Pied wagtail (female)

The pied wagtail with its characteristic waving tail often lives around buildings. As its names suggests, it is black and white.

You may also see grey wagtails for they are fond of water. They have a light-grey back (hence their name) and a yellow breast and belly which often causes them to be confused with the much yellower, and less common, yellow wagtail.

Notes

Notes

Black headed gull
Herring gulls
Mallards
Shelducks
Curlews
Sandpipers
Rabbits
Rock samphire
Thrift
Sea campion
Scurvy grass
Hermit crab

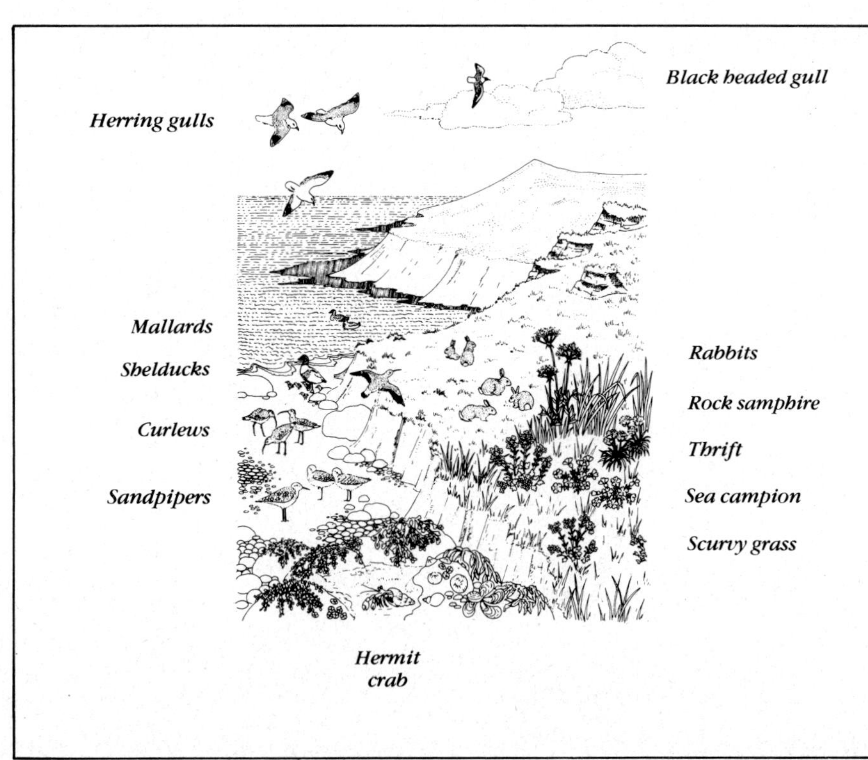

Sand Point

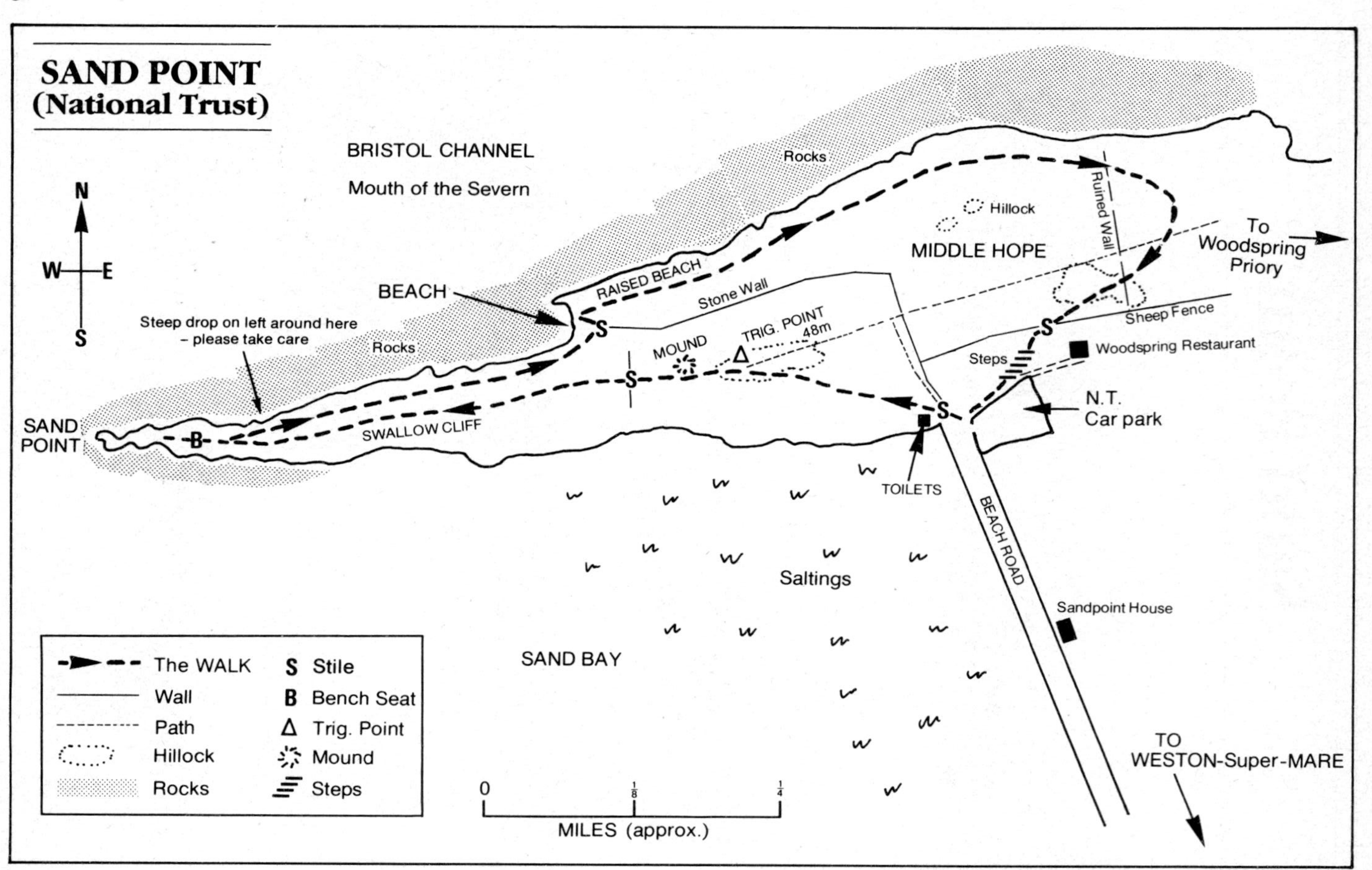

SAND POINT
(National Trust)
BRISTOL CHANNEL
Mouth of the Severn
N
W
E
S
BEACH
Steep drop on left around here
– please take care
Rocks
Rocks
RAISED BEACH
Stone Wall
TRIG. POINT
48m
MOUND
Hillock
MIDDLE HOPE
Ruined Wall
To
Woodspring
Priory
Sheep Fence
Woodspring Restaurant
Steps
N.T.
Car park
SAND
POINT
B
SWALLOW CLIFF
S
TOILETS
BEACH ROAD
Saltings
Sandpoint House
SAND BAY
TO
WESTON-Super-MARE
The WALK
Wall
Path
Hillock
Rocks
S Stile
B Bench Seat
Δ Trig. Point
Mound
Steps
0
1/8
1/4
MILES (approx.)

SAND POINT

O.S. ST36(330659) – Coastal walk

This walk will take you to the end of the northernmost of three finger-like promontories – Brean Down, Worlebury Hill and Sand Point – which project into the Bristol Channel. Being limestone, the walk should be fairly dry underfoot although, as it is exposed and can be very windy, a warm windproof jacket may be needed. The walk is about 2½ miles long and is quite steep in parts.

After leaving the National Trust car park, cross the lane and climb the stile to your right. Mount the steps and bear left where the path forks on either side of the wall.

Old man's beard grows over the bushes on the left of the path. It takes its name from its fluffy silvery seedheads whose windborne seeds are scattered when they ripen in autumn. In woodland this plant grows strongly, climbing quite tall trees towards the light and old stems often hang down like the lianas that Tarzan swings on – although old man's beard is generally not strong enough for such gymnastics. It is a good indicator of limestone, the hard light-grey rock from which Sand Point is formed.

Old man's beard seedhead

The view from this side of the Point is very fine with Weston Woods clothing the north side of Worlebury Hill, Birnbeck pier jutting from Anchor Head at its westernmost point and the two islands of Steep Holm and Flat Holm standing out of the waters of the Bristol Channel. Further along the coast is Brean Down and in the distance the north coast of Somerset.

Nearer at hand, the green area at the bottom of the cliffs is a small section of saltmarsh on which *glasswort* grows. It is a succulent-like plant with fleshy stems and leaves which vary in colour from green to red. Glasswort is grazed readily by domestic animals and is said to be the major dietary item of the white horses and black bulls of the extensive saltmarshes in the Camargue in the south of France. Farmers tend to like saltmarsh grazing, especially for sheep, as an occasional flooding by salt water kills the parasites which lurk in frequently-used pastures. This small area is not large enough for grazing but is used by wading birds which spread onto the large expanse of mud flats exposed when the tide is out.

The path leads out onto a clearing carpeted with short grass and surmounted by a concrete triangulation point (OSBM 3269).

The fine turf here is grazed largely by *rabbits* – a mammal popular in literature but unpopular in agriculture. Before myxomatosis spread so rapidly in the mid-fifties rabbits were extremely common, eating crops but also keeping areas of grassland like this clear of bushes, brambles and trees. Only thirty years ago there was far less undergrowth than today and pictures of places like Cheddar Gorge taken at that time clearly show this. It is on these stretches of short turf that many of our limestone flowers grow so well. Constant cutting back of the bushes and scrub is the only way to conserve such plants and nowadays the teeth of rabbits are replaced by the sickles and saws of conservation volunteers.

Green food presents the plant-eaters (herbivores) with something of a problem for, unless they can break down the cellulose parts of the plant, the food they eat is almost valueless. Cows get over this by having four stomachs, swallowing their food as they graze and later bringing it up in balls of cud to chew at leisure. Rabbits approach the problem differently. Part of the lower half of their gut (caecum) is a dead-end terminating in the appendix. This contains large quantities of bacteria which feed on the green plants which the rabbit eats. As digestion continues, some of these bacteria are swept out and are eventually excreted in soft membrane-covered pellets. At certain times of the day, the rabbit produces these droppings which are different from the fairly-hard brown fibrous balls you often see in small heaps outside their holes. The soft pellets are loaded with bacteria from the caecum and are thus very rich in protein. The rabbit immediately eats them. This activity is called coprophagy and is necessary because the food value of the soft pellets has to be absorbed by the upper part of the rabbit's digestive system although it only becomes available in the lower half.

A doe rabbit can, theoretically, mother or grandmother over 40 young in any year. The doe has no 'season' and conception is stimulated by the act of mating. Although born blind and naked a young rabbit reaches sexual maturity within 12 weeks.

Cross the green and follow the path via the stile to the Point.

Three plants are worth looking out for here and I have particularly chosen coastal species. The rounded pink flower heads of *thrift* may be seen from April to mid-summer growing on stems from its green cushion of leaves and, even in October, I have spotted the pale skeletons of flower-heads still on the plant. It was once pictured on the old twelve-sided threepenny piece because of its name. *Rock samphire* grows here too. It has light-green fleshy leaves which, like those of glasswort, are a frequent feature of plants which have to survive in a salty atmosphere and pale-yellow flowers appearing between July and the autumn. It is a member of the carrot family and, although its roots are not eaten, the leaves and stems were once cooked and consumed like asparagus.

Pink thrift grows from a cushion of vivid-green leaves

Light-green fleshy leaves and pale-yellow flowers are the hallmarks of rock samphire

Scurvy grass with its rounded leaves often grow in gaps in rocks

The third plant is also edible and its rounded green leaves can often be observed in gaps in the rocks. This is *scurvy grass* – it is not a grass despite its name – which has been eaten in the past by sailors who found it very effective in combating scurvy.

The sloping rocks on the south side are clearly coloured in bands, the topmost being yellow before changing to a strip of black above the seaweed growth. This does not result from natural colouring or tar stains but derives from a covering of lichen. The yellow variety is *caloplaca thallincola* which commonly grows above the high-water mark and the black one is *verrucaria maura* which is abundant at the high-water mark.

It is surprising how many outside surfaces support lichens and there are few exposed rocks where you can actually see much of the stone itself. You may come across several species during these walks especially on branches of bushes and on stone walls. Lichens are very good monitors of pollution; they are practically absent in some industrial areas and yet grow luxuriantly in the remote rural parts of Scotland. I find the biggest difficulty with lichens is their names for they do not often have common English ones. If you want to know more about them, do read the lichen book mentioned in the bibliography.

Lichens are a fascinating mixture of a fungus and an alga. They pair up to form a symbiotic relationship – each benefiting from the partnership and only survive because of it.

Return past the bench-seat and bear to the left along the cliff top path but take care as the path is quite narrow with a steep drop on your left.

One of my favourite maritime plants grows on the cliff-edge here and its white flowers with blushing pink-tinged sepal tube are around from May until September although the dried sepal tube can be seen after this. It is *sea campion*, a relative of *bladder campion*. Not only will it tolerate a salty atmosphere, it is also prepared to grow in the polluted soil of waste heaps which are found around old lead mines. Those near Priddy are a fine example.

Follow the path to the wall and climb over the stile.

The grassy area on which you are now standing is a raised beach. This was a beach before the last ice-age when the sea-level was about 5m. (16ft) higher than at present – the subsequent glacial period causing the sea-level to fall. The raised beach gradually soiled over and now supports grass rather than seaweed.

Climb down onto the seashore on your left.

When you first reach the beach, on your left, the rock can be be clearly seen in layers. The grey rock is limestone and was formed under a warm shallow sea where large quantities of shellfish were present. As these animals died their hard outside cases fell to the sea-bed and slowly built up there among the silts to form limestone.

As the rock was still being formed, a number of volcanic eruptions took place forcing molten lava out over the sea-bed where it cooled rapidly into rounded forms called 'pillows'. The lava, now a rock called olivine basalt, is only found towards the western end of the Point but here you can see layers of tuffs, a soft kind of volcanic fragmentary rock, which make the reddish-brown bands – in some parts veined white with calcite. You can pick up water-worn lumps on the beach here and they remind me a little of faggots wrapped in caul fat.

SAND POINT SOIL/ROCK PROFILE

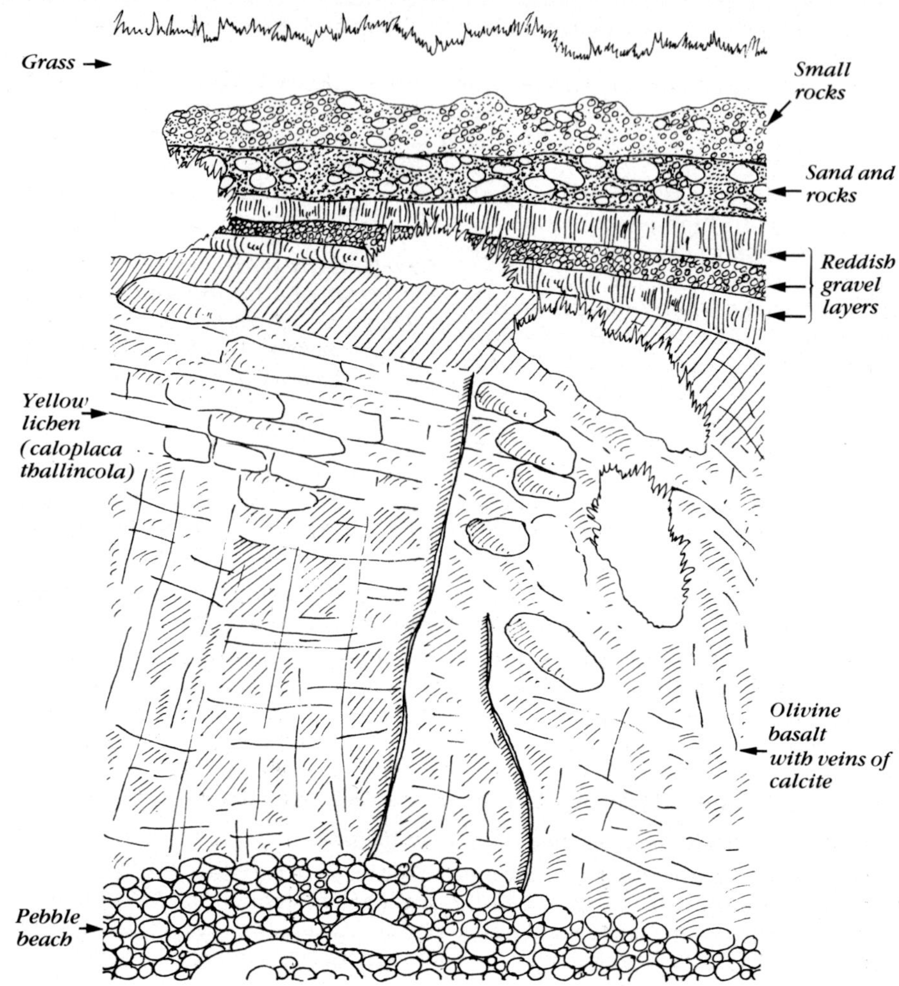

The Bristol Channel has an approximate rise and fall of 47ft which makes it second only in the world to the St. Lawrence river in Canada.

If the tide is out you can go down over the rocks here but beware of the slippery seaweeds. These algae are often given scant attention but are worth looking at, especially as three types of wrack found here are easy to tell apart. Generally, the various species live in different belts (zones) down the shore as each requires more or less time in water and in air. Strangely enough, the standard zoning is quite mixed up here and it is believed that this may be to do with the high tidal range or the quantity of sediments in the water of the Bristol Channel.

Flat wrack is without any air sacs and the end of each flat stem is divided and may be swollen. *Egg wrack* has single air sacs in the middle of each frond which has no midrib. Some of these bladders are very large and will pop when you tread on them. Finally, there is *bladder wrack* itself with a midrib and neat bladders on either side, usually in pairs. Hidden in deep recesses under these seaweeds you may make other interesting finds. At the very least, by lifting back the fronds, you should come across some good fossils such as small shellfish and even the spiral shape of an ammonite.

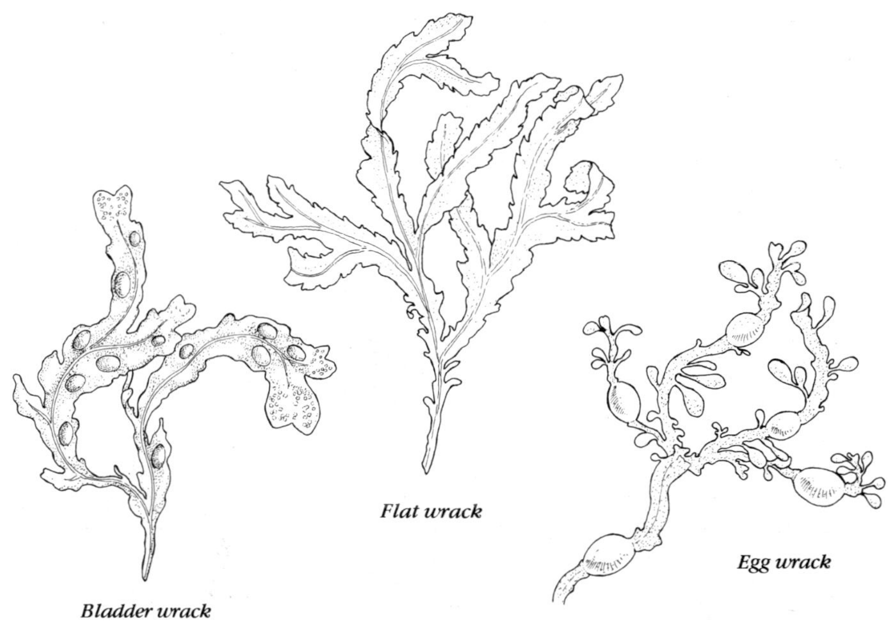

Flat wrack

Egg wrack

Bladder wrack

Hermit crabs are another favourite of mine. An apparently empty winkle or whelk shell inspected more closely may reveal a small crab's claw blocking the entrance. If you put the shell down and watch quietly, the occupant will eventually emerge and scuttle away with its borrowed home. As hermit crabs grow, their shell – being another creature's skeleton – does not grow with them. They have to look for a larger shell to protect their soft, fleshy and vulnerable tail and, in time, they will move up from a large winkle to a small whelk shell.

Hermit crab in a whelk shell. Its right claw is larger and closes the entrance against enemies when the crab is inside.

The *dog whelk* has only recently come to live this far up the Channel, for previously it was found only as far east as Blue Anchor near Minehead. Whelks are carnivores (meat-eaters) and the main prey of the dog whelk is the barnacle. Barnacles are small light-grey domed shells that often cover rocks so completely that there is hardly a space between them. They can crowd over 30,000 into a square yard and, not surprisingly, are the most common animal on rocky shores. They also cling to piers and even to the bottom of boats necessitating in their hulls having to be scraped regularly. Although they look like shellfish, possibly smaller versions of the limpet, they are in fact relatives of shrimps and crabs. If you inspect their shells carefully you will see that it is not all in one piece but is constructed of a number of plates. The *acorn barnacle*, as it is properly known, is able to open a trapdoor at the top of its body and protrude a number of feathery appendages which are continually pushed out and pulled in, hopefully catching small marine prey on the way. British acorn barnacles have six plates surrounding the trapdoor. During the mid-forties, an Australian barnacle started to colonise the south coast, gradually spreading westwards around Lands End and back up towards Bristol. It can be distinguished from the British species by the fact that it has only four plates around the opening.

British acorn barnacle with 6 plates

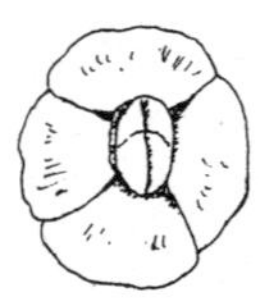

Australian acorn barnacle with 4 plates

Following the spread of the Australian version came the *dog whelk* for, as its food increased, so it was able to extend its range. Australian barnacles have now spread so prolifically that it is believed they may become the most common of the species around Britain. Whelks, unlike many carnivores, do not have to do much running about to catch their prey. Instead, they just crawl over to a patch of barnacles and force their feeding tube through the trapdoor of one, pour in digestive juices and suck out the contents to leave an empty shell. Indeed, you may find such empty shells, the four or six plates still in place but the trapdoor gone, stuck to the rocks on the shore. There are some varieties of sea shells illustrated on page 116.

Return to the shingle and climb back onto the raised beach, walking along between the shore and the stone wall.

On the far side of the stone wall is a large patch of *elder* bushes. These should not be confused with alders which are trees, generally found near streams for, although they may grow tall and stout, elders could never be called trees. When young their stems are filled with a white pith and from these it is easy to make pea-shooters. It is this feature that gives the elder its name, a corruption of the Anglo-Saxon word for 'hollow tree'. As the bush ages, its stem develops into a hard white wood at one time carved into any instrument needing a point such as a comb or a fine pricker used by a watchmaker. Like the rowan, it has a great tradition in folklore and to burn elder wood on the fire is said to bring bad spirits into the house.

Elder is one of the first plants to push out new leaves in the spring and is an early sign of warmer days to come. Although prompt with its leaves, elder flowers, in their great creamy-white clusters and with their heavy scent, do not appear until May or June. Some people make them into wine but I prefer elderflower 'champagne' myself, because it is ready to drink very quickly and it is so refreshing on hot days.

Elder flowers, leaves and berries

Elderberries follow soon after the flowers and a good year will see bushes laden with a burden of fruit at the end of August and in September. Then they are especially favoured by *starlings* who gather in their branches in large clamorous flocks. The juicy fruits can be made into more wine or used to flavour pies and jellies.

Elder bushes are often an indicator of badgers' setts as they like to grow on disturbed ground and the soil around a sett is turned over at frequent intervals either from new digging or by the inhabitants searching for food. Rabbits, which sometimes share setts or live in the same area, do not like to eat the leaves and shoots and so they are allowed to sprout unmolested. As badgers eat the berries, whose seeds pass through the animal without damage, elders will sometimes grow from dung deposited near the sett.

Badgers make good use of the elder, particularly in clay areas, for they clean mud from their claws on its thick soft yellow-grey bark. Whether they do this because the elder happens to be handy or because the texture of its bark suits their purpose is difficult to say but it is common to find the trunks of bushes which grow near setts to be deeply scored by the long claws of a badger's forefoot.

At the end of the wall, the pasture runs from the raised beach up the steep grassy hillside which has been terraced into horizontal paths by the passage of many sheep. Unless running in fear few domestic animals will go straight up or down a slope such as this but will either follow the contours or take a zig-zag course to avoid falling on the slippery turf.

Duck (left) and drake mallard in breeding plumage

Out at sea, *mallards* can often be spotted sometimes in groups or 'rafts'. These are very common ducks and are probably the best known of all duck species because they turn up in parks with ponds and almost any kind of waterside area. They are the ducks that children 'go and feed'. For most of the year the drake (male) is brightly plumaged with a bottle-green head, chestnut breast, blue flashes on his wings and a curly tail. In late July and August though, mallards moult to renew their feathers and, like many water-birds, lose all their flight feathers at once. At this time, the male takes on the drab brown plumage of the female so as to escape detection by camouflage. They usually take up residence in saltmarshes like those on the south side of Sand Point.

In the winter, groups of mallard will form into courtship assemblies and at the instigation of one bird the whole party will indulge in a courtship display. The drakes perform one part of the dance which is a complicated ritual involving a lot of splashing, whistling and quacking while the females incite them, each possibly choosing a particular mate which she tries to lead out of the group.

As you make your way along the raised beach, a large round hillock appears on your right with a green track cutting the left-hand shoulder of the rise. Cross the ruined wall which, at its seaward end, can only be identifed by bramble and elder bushes although more stones are visible on the hillside. Bear right and climb up the green track.

On a clear day the view up the Channel from here is superb. Clevedon nestles into the hills on the right with its pier jutting out to sea. In the distance the graceful outlines of the Severn Bridge can be seen spanning, in single sweep of over a mile, the waters of the Bristol Channel. Inland of Clevedon, the M5 motorway runs down through a cleft in Tickenham Hill after leaving one of the most impressive pieces of highway engineering in Britain and descends to the low flat moors, barely climbing again until south of Bridgwater.

When you can see the sheep fence running along to your right, turn sharp right parallel to the fence.

Woodspring Priory with its stone tower can be seen down on your left. The Priory was begun here in the 1220s in a chapel dedicated to St. Thomas Becket. It seems that the manor at 'Worspring' was owned by one of Becket's murderers and that his grandson founded the Priory by way of penance. There was always a shortage of money and it took many years to build; the chancel and the Lady Chapel were not completed for a hundred years. Things looked up during the next century though and a barn, church and hospital were built.

By this time Henry VIII was already in dispute with Rome but rather than argue with the King, the whole community (all eight of them) signed the document acknowledging the King as Supreme Head of the Church. Craftily, however, they had already disposed of most of the Priory lands. The community was finally suppressed two years later in 1536.

The Priory buildings were used mainly for agricultural purposes until the end of the last century when they became a golf club. At the end of the World War I they were bought for conversion to a hotel but luckily nothing came of this scheme and the National Trust finally bought the estate in order to conserve it.

Unfortunately it is not possible to reach the Priory from here. You have to go back towards Weston-super-Mare and then return on a road parallel to Sand Bay.

Go back across the old wall which is in a better state up here and walk towards Birnbeck Pier in the distance and thus to a stile in the sheep fence and descend the steps. At the bottom, turn right onto the lane, and return to the car park.

Where you leave the track, a number of *white poplars* have been planted. These trees are commonly used as wind-breaks in sandy areas as they put out suckers from the roots and so rapidly establish a good number of plants to provide shelter. They have leaves with up to three lobes which are glossy dark-green on the upper surface and have a white matted underside, from which they take their name.

White poplar leaf

If you like seaside walks, try the Berrow walk, described on page 93.

Notes

Notes

Great spotted woodpecker
Goldcrest
Blue tit on beech
Hart's tongue fern
Badgers
Grey squirrel
Coal tit
Roe deer
Bluebell
Dormouse on hazel
Primrose
Great tit
Woodmouse

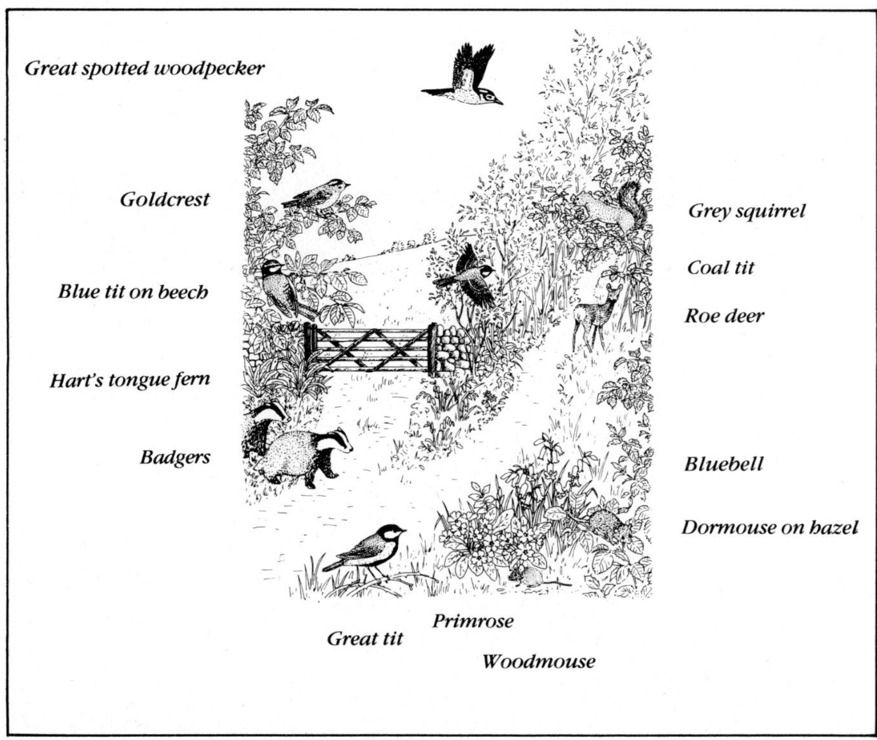

Bourton Combe

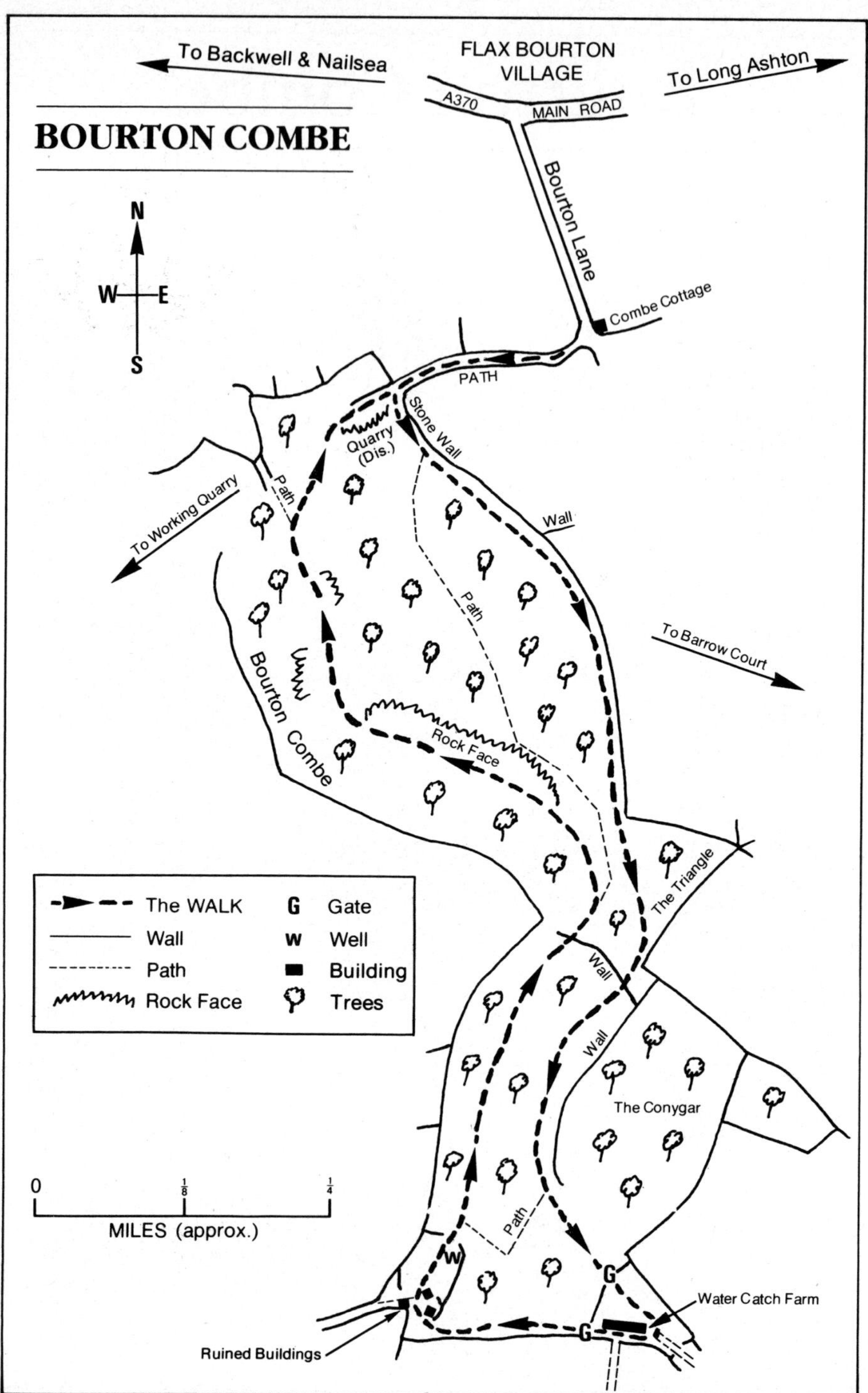
BOURTON COMBE
FLAX BOURTON VILLAGE
To Backwell & Nailsea
To Long Ashton
A370
MAIN ROAD
Bourton Lane
Combe Cottage
N
W
E
S
PATH
Stone Wall
Quarry (Dis.)
Path
To Working Quarry
Wall
Path
To Barrow Court
Bourton Combe
Rock Face
The Triangle
Wall
Wall
The Conygar
Path
W
G
G
Water Catch Farm
Ruined Buildings
The WALK
Wall
Path
Rock Face
G Gate
W Well
Building
Trees
0
1/8
1/4
MILES (approx.)

BOURTON COMBE

O.S. ST56(508690) – Woodland walk

It can be a damp place this, so wellies are advisable unless it has been fairly dry for some time. Although not flat, there are no steep hills but the rocks underfoot can make the going a bit rough – about two and a half miles in all.

If driving leave your vehicle at the top end of the Bourton Combe Lane. Take the public footpath to the right, signposted 'Barrow Common'.

On this first corner is a group of oak trees which, in autumn, produce acorns in woolly acorn cups. They are *Turkey oaks* and are of southern European origin. This walk will give you the opportunity to compare them with the so-called *English (pedunculate) oak*. The leaves of the Turkey oak have lobes which are more pointed than those of the native species and the acorn cups of the pedunculate oak are knobbly rather than woolly. Turkey oaks were originally introduced for their rapid growth and have become naturalised in a number of places. If you can find a Turkey oak leaf on the ground take it with you to compare with those of the pedunculate oak later on.

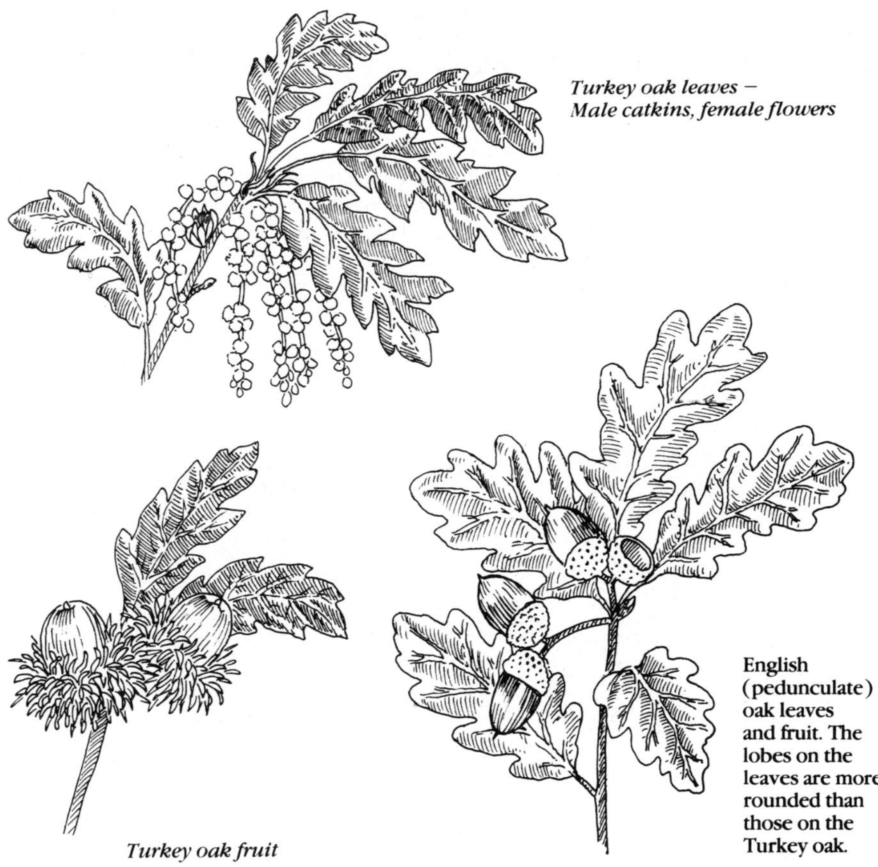

Turkey oak leaves – Male catkins, female flowers

Turkey oak fruit

English (pedunculate) oak leaves and fruit. The lobes on the leaves are more rounded than those on the Turkey oak.

The path you are following lies at the bottom of a north-facing slope and is very shaded from the sun, this causes it to be damp and therefore a good place for ferns to grow. The most noticeable species here is *hart's tongue fern* with its long dark-green shiny fronds. These are especially beautiful when fresh and bright in spring as they gradually uncoil. Their name presumably originates from their resemblance to the tongue of a hart or deer.

Also along here you should come across *soft shield ferns*. This species is more typically fern-like in appearance and can be identified by its 'thumbs'. One of the two leaflets next to the stalk of the frond is larger than the other and sticks out like a thumb. If you look more closely, you can see a small 'thumb' at the base of each leaflet as well. On the underside of the leaflets, you may see rows of spores which are eventually scattered from the plant to produce new ferns. See illustrations of ferns on page 110.

There is a good opportunity here to look carefully at *ivy* leaves. Most people recognise ivy as having shiny dark-green five-lobed leaves and these are especially noticeable on strands of this climbing plant as they snake across the woodland floor seeking a tree to climb. Having found a suitable vertical surface, the plant attaches itself with a special glue and climbs upwards. It uses trees only for support and is not a parasite in any way. Once it reaches a site that has good light, sometimes fifty feet above the ground, its leaves become more oval with a point and at this stage it produces flowers. Unlike most other plants, the ivy waits until autumn to do so and thus encourages the attentions of many late flying insects for whom the choice of nectar-bearing flowers is now very limited. It has a very heady scent, slightly reminiscent of the musky smell of otters.

Ivy berries do not ripen fully until early spring when their black bunches are much beloved by birds – who are, by now, very short of food. Although it lives in an apparently hostile environment – closely shaded by forest trees – by reversing the seasons, ivy has made itself needed because of a lack of alternatives, and is more visible because trees have lost their leaves.

Ivy leaves and flowers – The flowers do not come out until autumn

Pass through the stone wall with a gatepost on the left.

On the right here is a fine specimen of a pedunculate oak. It is an easily-recognisable tree because of its distinctive leaves and acorns, but even without these, in the middle of winter, this oak has a very angular shape with lots of 'elbows' to its branches. There are two common native oaks, the pedunculate and the *sessile*. On the former the acorns are on long stalks (peduncles) while on the latter the acorn cups are stalkless and bunch together as a result.

Turn left here and walk up the path between the field and the wood.

The first area of woodland consists of old coppiced *hazel* – hazel bushes which have been continually cut down at about seven-year intervals and then allowed to grow new stems from the stump or 'stool'. The crop of straight stems was once of enormous economic importance in the countryside. They were employed for everything from pea and bean sticks to making hurdles and were also extensively used for making charcoal, not because our forebears had many barbecues, but used for any process requiring extreme heat such as steel-making. Nowadays almost all of these needs are fulfilled in other, more modern, ways and hazel coppicing is a dying skill.

From the point of view of conservation this is most unfortunate as not only does hazel coppice tend to have a particularly rich array of flowers, but it is also the major habitat of the *dormouse* which is found in this area. This gingery furry-tailed little animal is not very common, emerging only at night to feed on vegetable food. Unfortunately, the demise of the hazel coppice could mean an increasing scarcity of dormice which would be very sad as they are delightful animals.

The dormouse is becoming increasingly scarce as hazel coppicing is dying out

You can play nature detective and see what small mammals are in this wood by inspecting hazel nuts. If you can find a nut shell with a hole neatly chiselled out of one side and kernel missing, the feeder could be one of three animals: the *woodmouse*, the *bank vole* or, more unusually, the dormouse.

Look carefully at the rim of the hole as marks on both the edge of the hole and the shell surface are indications of woodmice at work. The bank vole makes no marks on the shell surface, only around the edge of the hole, while the dormouse leaves swirl marks on the shell surface but smooths out the inside edge of the shell. Search for these shells along the edge of the path, using a magnifying glass if necessary to check the rim of the hole (see illustrations on page 113).

The catkins of hazel are present throughout the winter in a tight retraced form and early in spring they elongate to proper 'lambs' tails. At this time of the year look out for the tiny red female flowers which will be pollinated by the yellow pollen which the male catkins shed.

The plants in deciduous woodland have evolved to bloom early from bulbs or rhizomes. This foodstore gives them a boost in spring to push out flowers and leaves before the foliage grows on the trees overhead and deprives them of light – *bluebells* are a good example of this. Here, you may see *dogs mercury* – a plant with a spike of green flowers – and possibly *primroses*, *wood anemones* with their delicate white flowers, and *ramsons* (wild garlic) which have extremely pungent foliage.

In spite of their evolutionary efforts, these flowers are unlikely to grow under the large *beech* tree (along the path on your right) as the foliage of this tree is generally so dense as to shade out completely plants trying to grow beneath. The tree can be identified in the winter by the smooth grey bark on its branches and its brown cigar-shaped buds. Spring time sees delicate downy light-green leaves which gradually darken during summer and then turn golden brown in autumn. The beech seed is called mast and consists of triangular nuts held in a case covered with soft spines. The mast is much loved by squirrels and woodmice as well as numerous birds. There are *sycamore* trees here too, and in summer it is interesting to check their five-lobed leaves for black spots. These are called 'tar spots' and are caused by a fungus.

Squirrels can damage sycamore trees by stripping their bark – often leaving it in tatters hanging down the tree. If the bark is removed all round the trunk the tree will die.

There are many signs of *badgers* in this wood. You may see feeding signs such as small excavations left after digging for worms, logs overturned or moss scratched up in search of beetles, roots dug up or even large holes left after a wasps' nest has been exhumed and eaten. In this case, the badger, which loves wasp grubs, does not follow the entrance hole into the nest because of the risk of receiving a sting on the nose. Instead, it digs straight down to the nest and relies on its thick coat to deter angry wasps. On the following day, all that remains is a large hole with a few pieces of papery nest and a number of disgruntled adult wasps buzzing around in the bottom.

Badger paths are very evident, trails of hard earth pounded over the centuries by generations of badgers. Where they lead under barbed-wire fences, badger hairs (white at each end and black in the middle) are often left clinging to the barbs and worth watching out for. Being fiercely territorial, as badgers are, their paths have great significance and lead from the main sett to outlying holes, to favourite feedings grounds or watering places, or perhaps around the perimeter itself. Not unnaturally, the animals resent any interruptions to their paths and when man builds a road across an existing path, they continue to follow their route even if the surface itself has changed completely. Nowadays, to avoid accidents, artificial badger tunnels have been built under many new roads.

It is possible that you may find a mark across the path with a scattering of grass and leaves on either side as if a dead body had been dragged into the wood – this is a badger bedding trail. Badgers being comfort-loving animals, like to tuck themselves up underground in a mass of grass and leaves. This bedding has to be renewed from time to time and badgers will then wander off to find suitable material to collect which they drag backwards to the sett by gripping it under their chin whilst holding it in place with their front paws. As one would expect, quite a lot of the carefully gathered vegetation spills out on the way or is snagged on roots or bushes and this is what you will see. You can just imagine the labours of the night and the grunting and shuffling sounds that accompany this activity.

The path levels out and at this point two tall *lime* trees can be found. The trees here show many of the typical features of limes: they are the tallest broad-leaved tree in most areas and these two are certainly large specimens. Around their

Badgers – Their biggest threat is man and many are killed on the road

base are dense masses of sprouting twigs and high in the branches are clumps of *mistletoe.*

The leaves of the lime are heart shaped and pointed and in summer can be shiny with honeydew from aphids. As anyone who has parked a car under a lime tree will know, this honeydew falls on everything beneath the tree and the spots turn black with *sooty-mould.* The leaves sometimes have *nail galls* attached to them which can be identified by their similarity to red dunces' caps.

The mistletoe that you can see in winter when the lime is bereft of leaves is a semi-parasitic plant. Its sticky white berries are rubbed into crevices in bark by birds trying to clean their bills. From here the plant sprouts, its branches divide, and divide again, to form the mistletoe bush – if that is what it can be called – so familiar to us all. The plant is either male or female and their flowers which appear in spring are wind-pollinated and the berries ripen in time for Christmas, when a sprig may be hung up for kissing beneath. This custom possibly comes from ancient fertility rites or perhaps to denote peace and hospitality.

Soon after passing the limes, you will come across a very large section of tree trunk on the right with a good crop of colourful bracket fungi of various species. At this point the wood extends out to the left into an area called The Triangle. Continue along the path through the remains of a wall into a mixture of trees which include *scots pine* and *larch* on the left. In the tops of these you can sometimes hear the high voices of tits. *Great tits* and *blue tits*, which come to garden bird-tables, will be present in mixed flocks with *coal tits*. The latter are slightly smaller than

Coal tit – These delightful little birds sometimes visit bird-tables

blue tits and have white cheeks and a white nape on a black head. They have quite long fine bills with which they probe bark and cones for insects. Sometimes tiny *goldcrests* will join these tit flocks. Although you may not see these birds immediately, if you stand still and keep quiet, looking up you should spot them flitting from one tree to to another.

Go through the gate and keep to the left of the farm buildings until you reach the end of them. Here, turn sharp right and, with the fields on your left, walk back past the other side of buildings and pass through the gate back into the woods.

There will be a number of large beech trees on the right before you come to two groups of ruined buildings. At the second group, opposite the old barn with stone steps, turn right into the combe again.

Pause here to look at the scots pine and the larch between the buildings. The larch is a particularly gnarled specimen and, without its needles, has the appearance of an old man with his back bent against the wind. A well and pump can be seen by the path here which presumably served the steading that once thrived at this point.

The vegetation in this early part of the combe is quite young and airy with spindly sycamore and *ash* trees reaching up for the light, while *rhododendrons* start to appear on the left. Although beautiful when in flower, these imports from

The brightly-coloured jay with its loud cackling call likes oak woods as it is very partial to acorns. In autumn it buries many as store against severe weather and those remaining undiscovered often take root as new oaks.

Green woodpeckers may be seen feeding on ant-hills on the ground

the Far East are disliked by naturalists because they quickly crowd out native species and can take over a wood completely.

Throughout the wood are hollow trees in various stages of decay and signs of woodpeckers are frequent. These birds are not known for being either quiet or drab. The *great spotted woodpecker* is a black and white bird with both sexes having a bright-red patch of feathers beneath their tail, and in the male, on the nape of the neck too. While the *green woodpecker* has similar crimson plumage, this time on its crown, its overall coloration is greeny-yellow. The great spotted woodpecker communicates by drumming on tree trunks, often choosing hollow trees which resonate better. The green woodpecker, on the other hand, drums rather less and is better known for its laughing cry which has earned it the nickname of 'yaffle'.

Woodpeckers have feet with two toes pointing forwards and two back so that they can grip more firmly to wood. Their tail feathers are stiff and act as a rigid third point of contact to enable the bird to have a solid base from which to chisel away at the timber.

Woodpeckers eat insects, chipping bark away to reach the invertebrates lurking beneath. Where it is impossible to reach their prey in this way, the woodpecker will probe under bark with its long barbed tongue to secure its meal. Green woodpeckers also feed on the ground and, by walking quietly, you may come across one hunting at an ant-hill whereupon it will fly off with its characteristic swooping flight and a cry of alarm.

The path forks here. Keep left to the down-hill arm.

Almost at once on the right is a large old pedunculate oak, the grandfather of the wood, with its boughs showing the typical angular 'elbows' and growing festoons of *polypody* ferns like something from a tropical rain-forest. This fern prefers dark shady north-facing woodlands where there is plenty of moisture. It suffers very badly in hot summers when even the mossy branches of trees like this dry up (see illustration page 110).

This is the most exciting part of the wood. Bright and picturesque on snowy days, it will be cool and shady in high summer for the main tree species here is the *yew*. These are some of the finest yews I know – beautiful trees and extremely old, whose bark turns a reddish-orange colour when wet. Often planted in churchyards, the yew has a significant place in Christian religion and is a symbol of life force. The tree itself is a good nesting site for many bird species and its berries are eaten by mammals as well as birds.

The ground is often damp here because of the shadiness of this deep combe and there will be many tracks in the soft earth. In particular, look out for the delicate cloven-hoofed footprints of the little roe deer (see page 115 for illustration), a russet-coloured animal little bigger than a red setter, that passes through this woodland from time to time.

Follow the path round to the right and uphill at the fork. Pass the disused quarry on your right and you will find yourself back at the pedunculate oak. Continue straight on to reach the metalled lane once more. Have a nice walk.

Roe deer – Dainty animals rarely seen in groups of more than three

Notes

Kestrel
Lapwing
Heron
Mute swans
Hare
Dunnock
Pied wagtail
Goldfinches on thistle
Goldcrest
Frog
Wren
Field vole
Pygmy shrew
Woodmouse
Bank vole on bramble

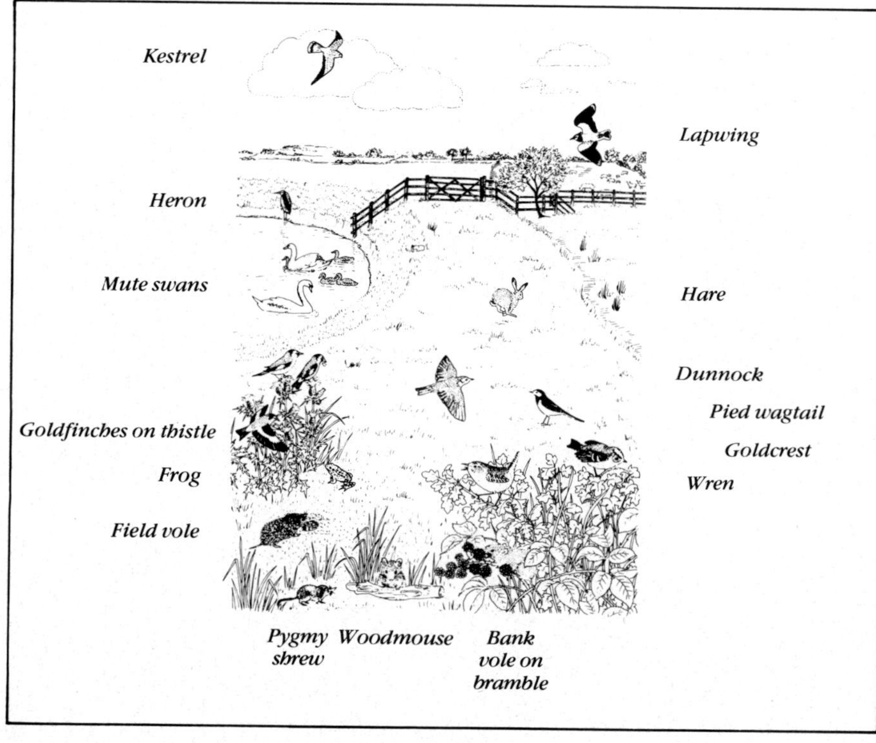

Yatton

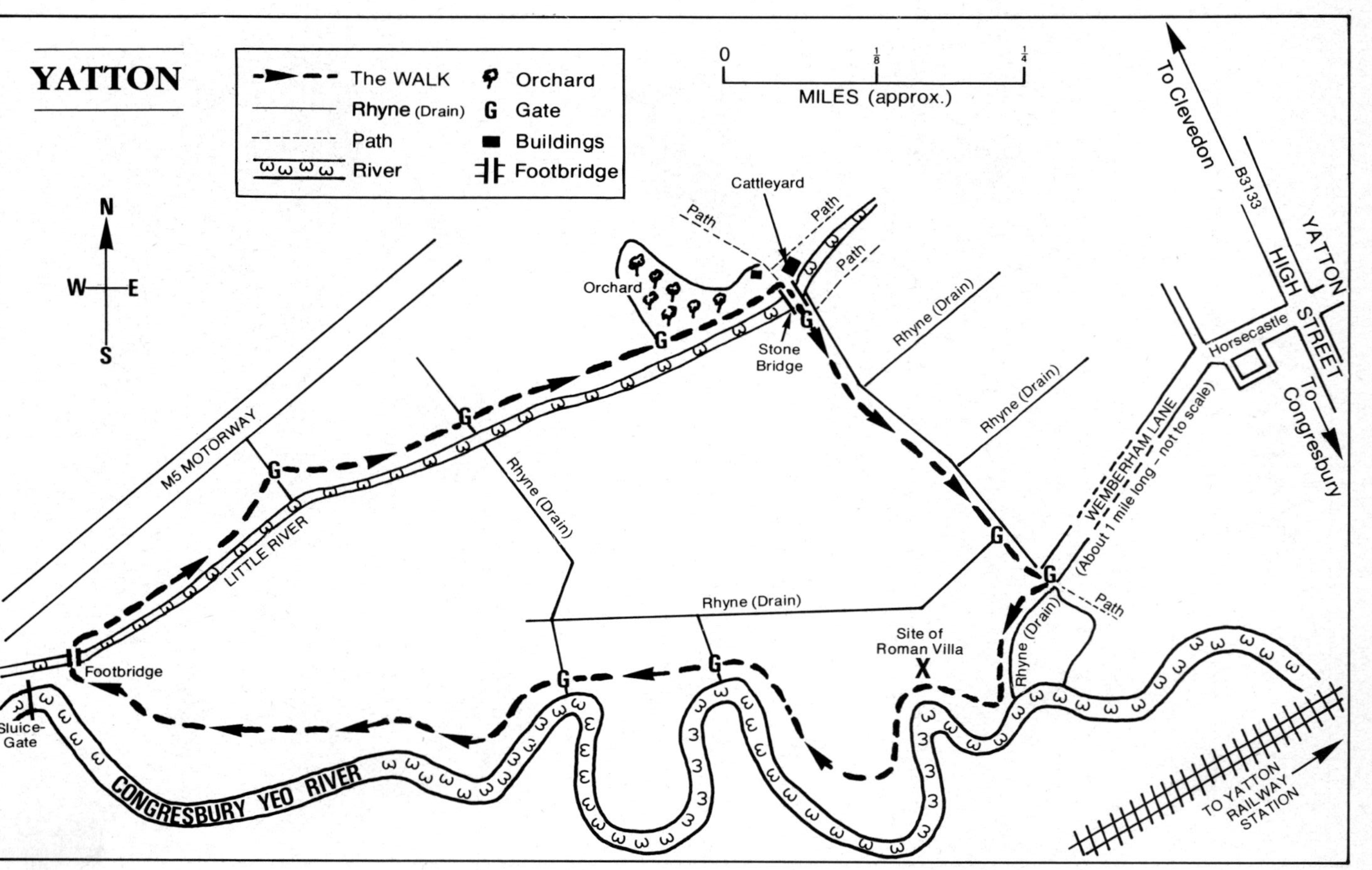
YATTON
The WALK
Orchard
Rhyne (Drain)
Gate
Path
Buildings
River
Footbridge
0
1/8
1/4
MILES (approx.)
N
W
E
S
To Clevedon
B3133
YATTON
HIGH STREET
Horsecastle
To Congresbury
Cattleyard
Path
Path
Path
Orchard
Stone Bridge
Rhyne (Drain)
Rhyne (Drain)
WEMBERHAM LANE
(About 1 mile long – not to scale)
M5 MOTORWAY
Rhyne (Drain)
LITTLE RIVER
Rhyne (Drain)
Path
Rhyne (Drain)
Site of Roman Villa
Footbridge
Sluice-Gate
CONGRESBURY YEO RIVER
TO YATTON RAILWAY STATION

YATTON O.S. ST46(408654) – Flat pasture land with rivers and rhynes

This is a flat walk which can be wet in winter. The route takes you across fields beside the Congresbury Yeo river to the M5 motorway and then back across these levels. The valley here has been used for communications since Roman times and, as well as the river, a modern motorway and a mainline railway pass very close by.

If parking a vehicle, do not block any gateways. Pass through the two gates at the end of the road and, walking on top of the bank, keep to the right of the hedge which surrounds the final stretch of the Wemberham Lane rhyne.

This sort of thick hedgerow is perfect for small birds like the *wren* and the *dunnock* (hedge-sparrow). Whilst the former is our smallest very common bird, the goldcrest and the firecrest, which are smaller still, are not as rare as were once thought. Wrens are pert little birds with brown speckled plumage and an upright tail. They are extremely noisy, scolding their enemies in cross tones from hedgebottoms and singing their very loud song with great gusto; a song which can be identified by the whirring sound at the end – like that of a clockwork motor running down. Male wrens build several nests in spring and their mates then choose the one they favour most. When hatched the young birds are reared sufficiently quickly for wrens to produce two broods in most years.

The maintenance of wren numbers in this way is important for, like all very small birds and mammals, they have a problem in keeping warm in winter because their body surface area is large in proportion to their volume. Many succumb during cold weather especially if there is prolonged snow and the wren's insect food is scarce.

In an attempt to keep warm in winter wrens will crowd together in roost sites. Up to 46 have been found in a single nest box.

The dunnock is larger than the wren but more retiring in its habits spending most of its time searching through the leaf-litter for invertebrates. Although called the hedge-sparrow, it is not related in any way to the sparrows which have the broad bills of seed-eaters whilst that of the dunnock is the slim beak of the insectivore. Its plumage provides excellent camouflage as its back feathers are mottled brown and black and those of its head, breast and underparts are grey. Dunnocks and wrens are frequent garden visitors but, as birds that feed on or

The wren is a little bird with a loud song

Dunnock (hedge-sparrow) A quiet secretive bird

near the ground and do not like to leave close cover, they are rarely seen on bird-tables although, strangely enough, both species utilise mine.

Follow the bank to the river and turn right to cut off the bend and walk across to meet the river again.

Here, on your right, looking down from the rise made by the bank, the ground is rather rough and bumpy and this area is the site of a roman villa. Although the Romans had occupied Britain in AD 43 this part of the country was not settled intensively until almost 250 years later. At that time Britain was in a state of some unrest and it is strange to find development on this scale under those circumstances. Some surmise that the occupiers were Romans displaced from France. In any event the villa, here at Wemberham, was a grand affair and one of the wealthiest in the area, which, being fertile, tended to have such agriculturally-based properties at fairly frequent intervals.

Wemberham villa was discovered in 1884 when land drains were being laid. Twelve rooms were found, forming only part of the house; six were floored with mosaics, four of which were patterned. The building consisted of two storeys and had the benefit of underfloor heating. I suspect that water levels were lower then – possibly by up to two feet – for it seems likely, from adjacent discoveries, that corn was grown here. The nearby river, the Congresbury Yeo, was navigable past this point thus providing easy transport for heavy or bulky goods from the villa's private landing point. If you would like to know more about Wemberham and the Roman occupation of the area, Woodspring Museum in Weston-super-Mare has displays including parts of the original mosaic floors.

Follow the river for a short way and then bear off right along the flood bank to cut off the corner of the river.

Field vole

At times *field voles* occupy this bank which must provide drier accommodation than its surroundings. These are timid little grey-brown mammals with blunt noses, furry ears and very short furred tails. You may see their holes in the ground, often with very short grass in the immediate vicinity. This is known as a 'vole garden' and is created by the vole itself who, too scared sometimes to wander far for food, will pop out of the entrance, nip off a grass-stem or other vegetation and retreat out of danger and into its burrow to feed. Field voles are probably the most strictly vegetarian of all the common small mammals and form the base diet of many carnivores, especially *foxes* and birds of prey. It is, therefore, hardly surprising that, living in such an open location, they do not like to venture far from safety.

Pass through the gate and note the hawthorn on the right which has been rubbed smooth by cattle. The bank forks at this point; take the right fork to cut off the next river corner.

You may see a *heron* here, either stalking with slow steps in the muddy edges of the river (look for its big tracks if you do not see the bird itself), standing motionless on the bank or even perched on the sluice-gate machinery in the distance. Although it is hard to believe, these large ungainly birds quite often

Heron chicks, if they feel threatened, will, as a form of defence, lean over the edge of the nest and regurgitate the remains of their last fishy meal over intruders – including people!

Heron

perch in trees and gather in a colony (heronry) to build their nests in the tops of a group of trees. Heronries will often have chicks in them as early as March.

Herons have a wide carnivorous diet which, apart from fish and eels, also includes frogs and small mammals which they catch by slow stealthy patient movements and a lightning devastating grab with their long dagger-like bill. Like many water birds, they often hunt at night and more than once I have been alarmed on a quiet moonlit walk by the sudden wingflaps of a departing heron. In spite of their high nesting habits, the herons' flights always appear heavy and laboured and often they come under attack, especially from *crows* and *rooks*. When this happens, they fly lower and lower until they almost touch the ground, often protesting with harsh cries of 'Fraa-ank fraa-ank'.

You may find a variety of plants growing on the dredgings from the river which are thrown up on the bank. In particular, *thistles* seem to thrive on this silty soil and in autumn their fluffy seed-heads will attract *goldfinches*.

Goldfinch on thistle. A flock of these birds is called a 'charm'

Continue along the path through another gate almost as far as the sluice-gate, turn sharp right and carefully cross the footbridge, turn right and follow the field boundary by the river to the gate. Pass through the gate and turn right to follow the field boundary once again.

The river is tidal as far as the sluice-gate and you may see the occasional seashore bird here as a result. The adjacent motorway as you walk beside the Little River is the M5. In an age of agricultural itensification and continuing destruction of wildlife habitats, motorway verges have provided small areas of respite for some species. Most people, when travelling along such roads, will have noticed a *kestrel* (windhover) maintaining station with its rapidly fluttering wings and broad tail as it searches the ground beneath for suitable prey. Kestrels will feed on beetles although they prefer mice or voles if they can find them. It seems to be a common fallacy that predators in general take items of prey much bigger than, in fact, they do. Thus foxes eat many voles and mice while a kestrel would find a rabbit impossible to deal with. I once watched a kestrel trying to fly off with a baby rabbit which had hardly grown its fur. Eventually the bird had to give up the unequal struggle for it was just not capable of carrying the weight. The rough and largely unmown motorway verges harbour many small mammals ensuring that their numbers remain fairly high thus attracting kestrels.

Kestrel

In addition to field voles, the verges are likely to provide a habitat for both *common* and *pygmy shrews*. These tiny insectivorous mammals with long quivering noses and tiny black eyes rush hither and thither in a constant search for food. Like the wren they suffer badly from heat loss and, to maintain their high metabolic rate and hence their body temperature, they have to eat something close to their own weight in invertebrate prey every day. Shrews are very quarrelsome creatures and when, fighting amongst themselves give high-pitched chirrupy, insect-like cries. These are audible to humans up to a certain age but become too high for older ears to hear. Other small mammals tend to avoid shrews; it is claimed that they possess toxic saliva which can be fatal to animals as small as mice. They rely a great deal on scent both to find their way around and to locate their prey, and they have scent-glands with which to mark their territories. These scent-glands make shrews distasteful to animals such as

Common shrew

Woodmouse

cats which will kill them but then abandon the corpses uneaten. Only owls are known to eat shrews with any regularity.

Where there is woodland adjacent to the motorway or the trees planted on the embankments are growing well, *woodmice* and *bank voles* are likely to be found. The bank vole is more gingery than the field vole and tends to like woodland; it climbs well and is fond of nuts and fruit. Woodmice – or 'fieldmice' as they are sometimes known – are small and brown with very long tails and with white underparts and a faint buff line running between their front legs. They, too, like to climb and will make winter stores of nuts or berries in old birds' nests or nest-boxes.

While motorway and roadside verges have provided very suitable habitats for all of these small mammals, they do have their disadvantages – a major one being discarded bottles and tins. All of these animals like to explore new holes and little entrances and empty bottles are prime candidates. The animals wriggles in through the neck and slides down inside only to find that it cannot climb back up the slippery glass and escape. Eventually it dies of starvation, or cold if there happens to be water at the bottom, and its body decomposes until only a few bones remain. I understand that the record for the number of skulls in a single bottle is 27; I once found 19 and, on many occasions, between six and ten skulls, so this is by no means an unusual occurrence.

Figures published a few years ago indicated that 9 million small mammals perish each year in 11 million or so discarded bottles and cans.

The Little River on your right with its damp banks is an ideal habitat for *frogs* and for *grass snakes* too. Frogs are amphibians which means they can live both on land and in the water. On land, they move about by leaping and trust to speed to escape danger. In water their powerful legs and large webbed feet will help them make a rapid getaway and they can remain hidden underwater with only their eyes and nostrils showing above the surface. Frogs have many predators so it is fortunate that they breed so prolifically, returning to the pond of their birth in February or March where each female lays up to 3,000 eggs, before the adults disperse.

Common frog

Grass snake

Frogs feed on insects – sometimes catching them with flick of their long sticky tongues – slugs, snails and worms. In autumn, when such prey becomes scarce, frogs go into hibernation, diving to the bottom of a pond or ditch and burying themselves in the mud there. Although they breathe through their nostrils on land, when submerged all winter in hibernation, they breathe through their skin which enables them to take in sufficient oxygen to survive in their torpid state.

One of the major predators of the frog is the grass snake. This reptile, which is harmless to humans, can be seen basking in the spring sunshine after its emergence from hibernation. Being cold-blooded animals they rely on the heat of the sun to warm their bodies and help the blood course round so that they have the energy to hunt. When basking, they flatten their bodies as much as possible in order to obtain the maximum benefit from this heat source. Grass snakes are olive-green in colour with black markings along their flanks; much the most noticeable identification mark is their yellow collar behind the head. The pupils of their eyes are round (those of the adder are vertical slits) and they grow up to three feet long.

Grass snakes, if unable to avoid capture, will feign death or exude a foul-smelling fluid which they tend to spray about when picked up. They eat frogs and newts, toads and fish and occasionally small mammals. The aquatic creatures are often caught in the water for the grass snake swims readily and is known in some places as the 'water snake'. The female lays soft-shelled eggs during the summer months in a manure heap or rotting vegetation as she relies on the temperature of their environment and the sun to incubate them, which can take up to ten weeks. It is this need for warmth for breeding that controls the distribution of the grass snake and it is rarely found north of the Scottish border.

Pass through the gate and keep to the bank of the Little River.

The path takes you through a gate into a cider orchard. Sadly for one of the area's well-known traditions, such orchards are becoming rather scarce as cider-making at the farm is a dying art. Such orchards are generally found near the farmsteading and are grubbed out to free additional land close to the farm, although this orchard, whilst it is near farm buildings, has no farmhouse nearby.

You may see a squirrel here for, apart from humans, they are the only wholly-diurnal (daytime active) British mammal. In autumn these animals enjoy the bounty of the orchard too. They are *grey squirrels*, rodents which came to this country from America. They tend to be more positively grey in winter, for, during summer months, their coats are often flecked and streaked with gingery-brown to such an extent that casual observers are sometimes fooled into thinking they have seen a red squirrel. Squirrels do not hibernate but they may spend several days in their nest (drey) if the the weather is especially bad. It is quite usual, however, to see the foraging signs of squirrels, or even the animals themselves, out in the snow on sunny days.

A squirrel's drey looks a little like a magpie's nest but normally the twigs from which it is constructed still have their leaves attached. This leafy ball is located in a fork of the tree, probably against the trunk, and is lined with grass, moss and leaves. Alternatively, the animals may make use of suitable hollow in a branch or trunk, and here they will breed. Female grey squirrels can have two litters in a year, one in the early spring and the other in the summer. The young are born blind, naked and deaf and take up to seven weeks to leave the nest. At first they have long thin tails and look distinctly rat-like; in fact foresters, who dislike

Grey squirrel and winter drey, lined with grass and shredded bark

Grey squirrels cache nuts and acorns in autumn against the winter but often forget their hiding places, thus unwittingly planting future trees. This, in some part, makes up for the damage they cause by bark-stripping.

squirrels, call them 'tree-rats'. Their bad reputation derives from their habit of stripping bark from trees. While red squirrels live in coniferous woodlands, the grey ones prefer deciduous hardwoods and cause considerable damage by bark stripping.

The scarring is bad enough and can lead to attack by disease; but worse still, the squirrel may strip the bark all round the trunk, killing the tree which may have been nurtured for 30 or 40 years. This naturally frustrates the forester.

Look for a drey in the row of trees next to the stream. Most of them are *horse-chestnuts* and can be recognised either by their leaves in 'hands' of five or seven, by their fruit (conkers) or by the scars on the twigs. These are reminiscent of horseshoe prints – complete with nail marks – and give the tree its name. The horse-chestnut is one of the first trees to change colour and lose its leaves in autumn. In spring the new leaves appear beautifully delicate as they break out of the well-known sticky buds, soon to be followed by white flowers which stand upright in bunches like candles on a Christmas tree. See illustrations on page 111.

Walk up to the buildings and turn right over the old stone bridge and through a gate. Note the unusual cattle-yard on your left with the whole of one side sloping down to the river. Follow the rhyne, keeping it to your left. (Do not cross the metal bridge.)

Look out for the land drains which spill into this rhyne draining the pasture on the far side. After rain they should be working hard, for this low-lying land waterlogs easily and the drains help to lengthen the time for which the fields can be used. Water in the soil tends to keep it cold and this suppresses plant growth; drainage makes it warmer earlier which enables the grass to grow sooner in spring.

Pass through the gate and keep to the side of the rhyne.

On rhynes as large as the Wemberham Lane rhyne there may be swans. These are *mute swans* with orange bills. The pen (female) has a small, black fleshy knob at the base of her beak while the cob (male) has a much larger one especially in spring. Although they seem common enough birds, their numbers have been depleted in recent years and are only maintained by swans coming from the Continent. The problem is one of lead poisoning. All birds eat small stones to help them with digestion – the stones collect in a muscular bag (gizzard) and grind up the food the bird has swallowed whole or in large lumps. But instead of stones, swans often pick up split-shot dropped by fishermen. This, of course, is quickly ground up by the gravel in the gizzard and the lead is absorbed into the bloodstream.

Mute swans – The female has a smaller black fleshy knob at the base of her beak

Lead-poisoned swans can be recognised by a bend in the neck which gradually becomes more acute until the bird finally dies. Fishermen and conservationists are taking this problem seriously and a weight made of an alternative material has been developed – hopefully lead weights will now be phased out.

Pass through the two gates and return to your starting point.

Notes

Notes

Magpies
Freisian cows
Ivy on dead elm
Blackbird on honeysuckle
Rabbits
Badgers
Palmate newts

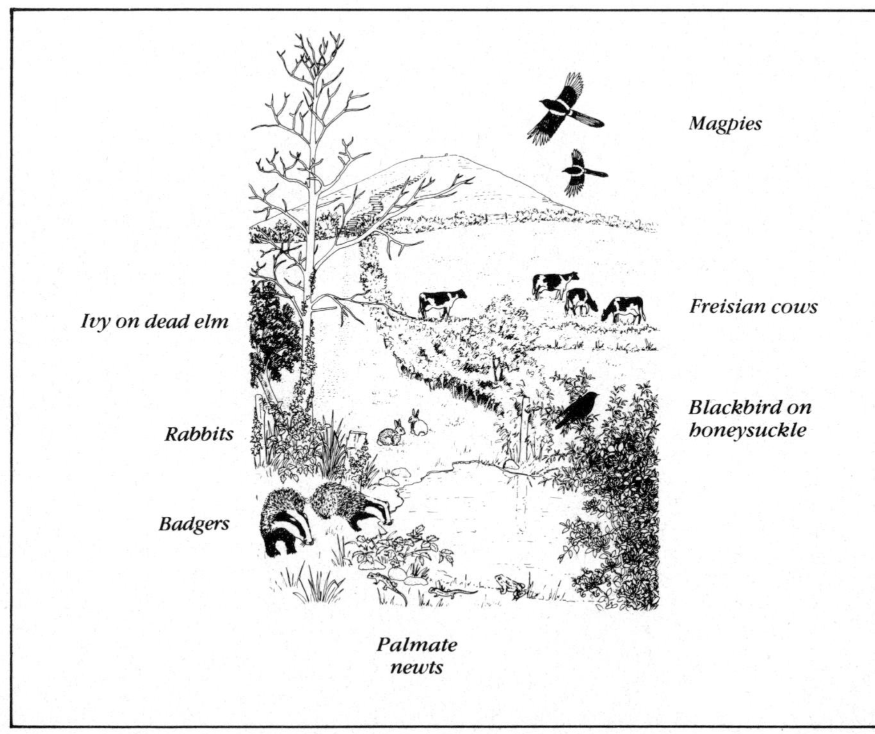

Brent Knoll

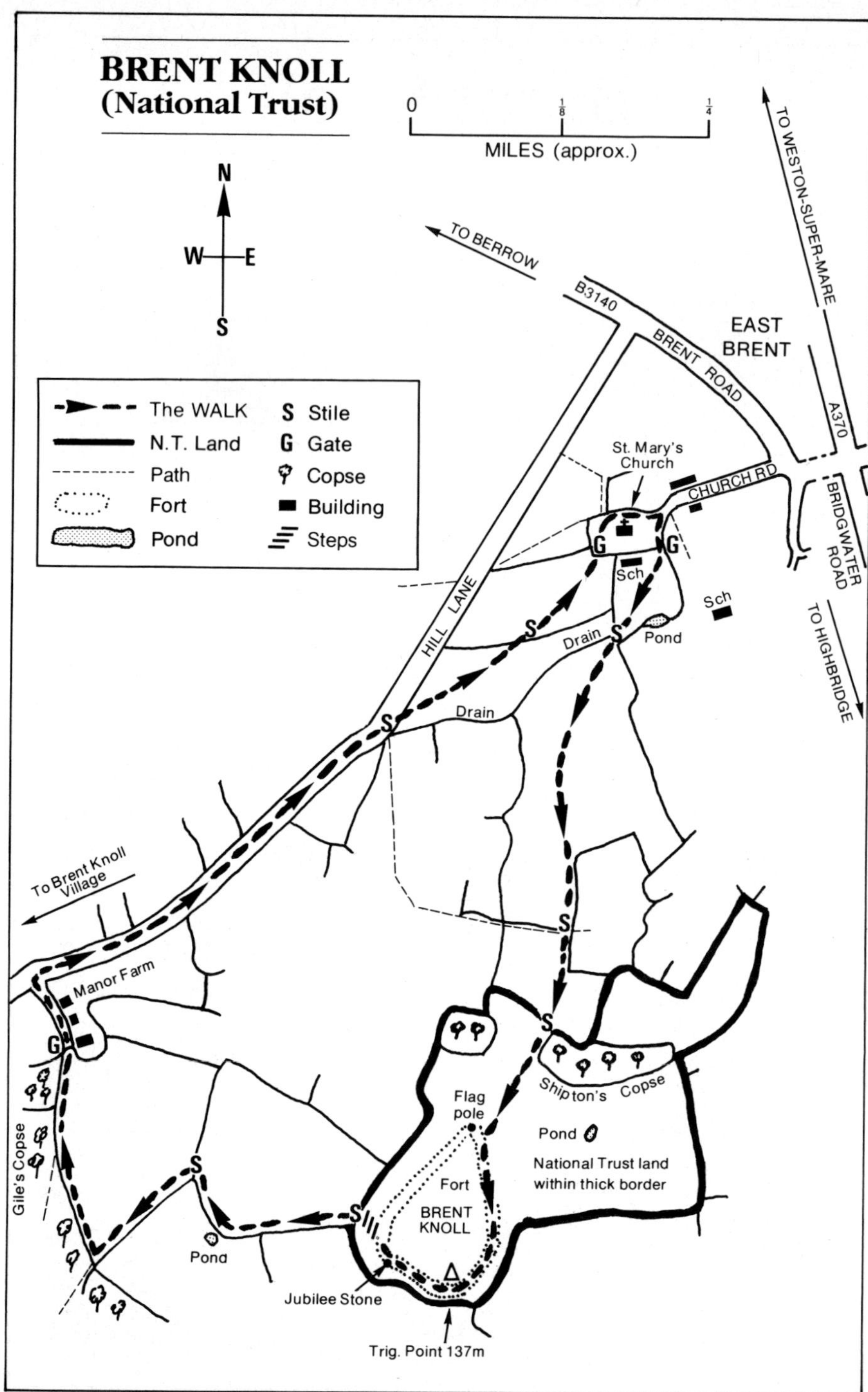
BRENT KNOLL
(National Trust)
0
1/8
1/4
MILES (approx.)
N
W
E
S
The WALK
N.T. Land
Path
Fort
Pond
S Stile
G Gate
Copse
Building
Steps
TO BERROW
B3140
BRENT ROAD
TO WESTON-SUPER-MARE
EAST BRENT
A370
St. Mary's Church
CHURCH RD
BRIDGWATER ROAD
TO HIGHBRIDGE
Sch
Sch
Pond
Drain
Drain
HILL LANE
To Brent Knoll Village
Manor Farm
Gile's Copse
Shipton's Copse
Flag pole
Pond
National Trust land within thick border
Fort
BRENT KNOLL
Pond
Jubilee Stone
Trig. Point 137m

BRENT KNOLL

O.S. ST35(344519) – Hilly walk with fine views

This walk of about two miles is very steep in places and you will climb over 400 feet in all; nevertheless the view is worth it. Brent Knoll rises like an island above the surrounding levels and is a well-known local landmark. The short well-nibbled grass is pleasant to walk on and is the main surface of the walk, which should be fairly dry even after damp weather.

Make your way into the churchyard and turn left before the church. A short diversion to the church porch and the church itself is, however, worthwhile in order to look for signs of bats.

Some species of bats make extensive use of church buildings because they are cool, dry and often clean. In some porches, bats can find their way into the roof space through quite tiny gaps around the ceiling, but I could find no signs of that here. More likely, at this church, they slip over the door and into the main building itself.

Signs of bats are easy to recognise – they leave small black droppings, a little like those of mice, except that bat droppings consist entirely of dried insect remains and will crumble to a powder if compressed. Look for them around the walls, especially in the corners, and on window-sills and seats.

Although there are more species of bats in Britain than any other species of mammal, these tiny animals are becoming increasingly rare. They are totally harmless and exceedingly well adapted to their way of life. Bats eat insects which they catch at night on the wing. If you can imagine trying to catch moths in woodland after dark with a butterfly net, you have some idea of the problems bats have to face.

The solution lies in a form of echo-location: they emit from their mouths, or in some cases their noses, high-pitched sounds which rebound off objects and are heard by the bats, thus enabling them to avoid colliding with trees and buildings whilst chasing their prey. They catch flying insects either in their mouths or in the sheet of skin stretched between their back legs and their tails.

In winter, when insects are scarce, bats go into hibernation, choosing somewhere cool like a cave or an old railway tunnel to sleep, often bunched together, hanging by their feet. Now their temperature falls to that of their surroundings, although never quite to freezing point, and their heart rate slows to around 30 beats a minute. They use very few resources and are usually able to survive on the fat they accumulate in autumn.

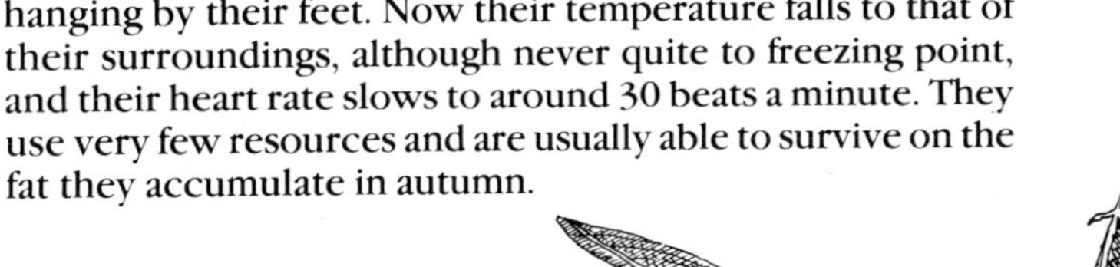

A pipistrelle, the smallest British bat, may eat over 3,500 insects a night in summer. At the height of the chase their temperature rises to 42°C and their heart races at 1,000 beats a minute.

Pipestrelle bat

Bats are enormously long lived for their size, and are known to survive for up to 30 years. They have few predators and so, unlike mice and voles which have a short lifespan and a high mortality rate and therefore breed prolifically, female bats average less than one offspring a year throughout their lives. During the last few years, their numbers have fallen dramatically and this comparatively slow rate of replacement means that, even if their difficulties were overcome now, it would be a long time before their population was fully re-established.

Some of the causes for the decline of bats will be seen on this walk. Basically there are two main factors: a loss of habitat for both daytime summer roosts and winter hibernation, and a shortage of food. Therefore both the animal and its home are totally protected by law.

Return to the path and turn right to cross the playground of the village school, then walk diagonally across the field towards the Knoll. Cross the stile and climb the ridge.

Brent Knoll, once known as the Insula Ranarum (Isle of Frogs) is not only an island in the literal sense, rising as it does from the wetlands of the Levels, but also in geological terms. It consists of a horizontal strata of Lias limestone and clay and was formed later than the nearby limestone Mendips. There is, thus, no truth in the legend that the hill was one of a number of spadefuls of soil thrown out by the Devil when he was cutting Cheddar Gorge! It is an area extremely rich in fossils and many have been picked up from the fields around the Knoll.

Leaves, flowers and fruit of common privet. A member of the olive family

Leaves, flowers and fruit of blackthorn. These are the sloes of sloe gin

Climb the next stile and walk up beside the hedge on your left.

Here, there are many dead *elms* left by the scourge of Dutch elm disease, and most are now just stumps. Although the felling of such notoriously fickle trees as elms (they tend to drop their branches without warning) is reasonable under the circumstances, it is unfortunate that the removal of old and dying trees has become a modern habit. This general 'tidying up' of the countryside often takes away hollow trees which are potential nesting sites for birds and, perhaps more importantly, would-be roosting places for bats.

The hedge contains a wide variety of hedgerow shrubs including *blackthorn*, *hawthorn*, *elder* and *privet*. Climbing over it may be *black bryony* which has shiny heart-shaped leaves and bunches of red berries in autumn. The leaves wither away and leave the poisonous berries strung over the hedge like clumps of red beads on a string.

Cross the stile to the next field entering National Trust land and start to climb the steepest part of the hill.

On the left here is a very steep bank – too steep for agricultural operations – which, as its name of Shipton's Copse suggests, once grew trees. The landowner has thoughtfully replanted this area and the young saplings are protected from the chiselling teeth of rabbits by plastic tree-guards. When they are fully grown they will help to repair the damage to the landscape caused by the death of so many elms.

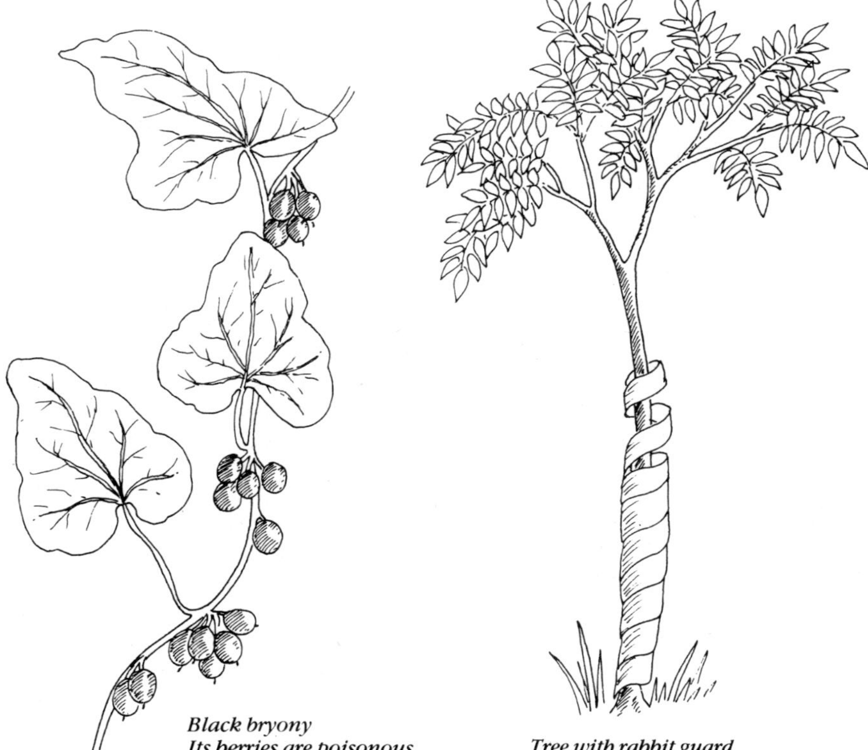

Black bryony
Its berries are poisonous

Tree with rabbit guard

The Knoll was acquired in 1979 by The National Trust for Places of Historic Interest or Natural Beauty. This organisation is not connected with the Government but is a charity set up in 1895 by three far-sighted Victorians – Octavia Hill, Sir Robert Hunter and the Reverend Hardwicke Rawnsley. The Trust has deliberately shied away from accepting government subsidy in order to preserve its independence and so relies on public donations to purchase and conserve areas like this for the benefit of all.

Climb the steepening slope to the top, pass the flagpole and walk round the summit in a clockwise direction.

From this side there is an excellent view of the motorway which is inescapable because of the surprising amount of noise that rises up the hill from it, even though it is over a mile away. It is interesting to notice just how much land the road occupies, especially at the nearby junction.

The triangulation point OSBM 3357 at 450 ft (137 m) is a good place to stop and admire the view. You will be by no means the first – Daniel Defoe, author of *Robinson Crusoe*, came here in the seventeenth century and John Wesley visited during the following century.

Looking south east, Glastonbury Tor should be clearly visible. Turning south and then south west will bring into view the Quantocks and Exmoor, the silvery river Parrett snaking into Bridgwater Bay, Burnham-on-Sea with its lighthouse and, immediately beneath, the strip of houses forming Brent Knoll village. These follow the road around the foot of the hill and cling to its lower slopes in order to gain just a few feet of higher ground above the wetness of the Levels. Out at sea the twin islands of Steep Holm and Flat Holm can be seen, supposedly two more of the Devil's spadefuls, while, more to the north, the church at Uphill perches on the edge of the quarried cliff fronting Weston-super-Mare. Turning almost a full circle, on the far side of the motorway, the great flank of Crook Peak can be seen; this is, however, the wrong angle from which to view the summit to see how this well-known local landmark gets its name.

As you would expect from such a steep and isolated hill, the top of Brent Knoll has served as a fortress for many over the centuries. Iron-age men created a hill fort here and remains of their pottery can be seen in Woodspring Museum, Weston-super-Mare; the Romans followed as discoveries of their coins indicate. During Arthurian times, Ider, one of his knights, is said to have killed three giants here. Although there may be some doubts about this, it is, nevertheless, certain that the summit has been quarried at various times, the most recent digging being during World War II when slit trenches were excavated around the summit plateau for the Home Guard.

The second marker stone records the various beacons and jubilee fires that have been held on this site from 1887 until the present day.

Continue around the hill to the top of the flight of steps.

Before your descent, pause a moment to view Manor Farm, the farmsteading below. The old stone farm buildings lie to the left while the modern grey-roofed and blue-walled construction to the right is a cubicle building. Cattle are kept in during the winter months because it is more convenient to feed them and prevents them churning up the wet pastures with their hooves. Until about 20 years ago, milking cows were kept in a cowshed, each one individually chained up, but then it was found to be cleaner and more efficient to put them in a cubicle house. Here, the cows are free to wander around, to eat silage or perhaps hay, or to lie down in one of the cubicles: individual bedding areas divided up with rails.

The farmer also makes silage: green grass which is cut, compacted and sealed to keep the air out to preserve it – a bit like a tin of peas. The most recent method is to make it into big cylindrical bales and store it individually in black polythene bags. You may see a stack of these bags at the farm.

Sacks of silage

Modern hay is made earlier than meadow hay used to be and silage is made earlier still. Many insects which breed in grassland need all summer to do so and the early cutting of the grass for silage prevents this. Bats, among other species, are thus deprived of an important food source which has contributed to their decline.

Descend the two flights of carefully-constructed steps to the stile. The National Trust has been especially thoughtful here and built a lift gate – a sort of portcullis, for dogs. Do keep your dog on a lead here as there may be stock on adjacent farmland. Descend the hill keeping close to the hedge on your left.

Just before the first gate in this hedge, ***honeysuckle*** is growing – a woody climber which binds spirally in a clockwise direction around any stem within reach. The flowers can be seen all summer but are most noticeable in July and September. They have a delightful fragrance and attract insects, particularly the *hawkmoth*, which has a long straw-like proboscis with which it sucks in nectar. Hawkmoths are well known for their ability to feed by hovering in front of flowers and inserting their proboscis whilst still airborne.

In autumn, honeysuckle produces lovely red berries with hard pips which are spread by birds eating the flesh. They are not good for humans and tasting them is inadvisable.

Privet hawkmoth feeding on honeysuckle – This plant has a beautiful scent on summer evenings

Follow the hedge to the bottom corner by the pond and turn right around the field boundary and left over the stile. Keep alongside the hedge on your left.

Extensive use of this area is made by *badgers* and there is probably a sett nearby. Their age-old paths of pounded earth can be seen leading through the hedge-bottom to the field here where they feed. One of their favourite foods is the earthworm which they seek at night when these creatures come out of their holes to find dead leaves or grasses. Sometimes the badger is able just to pick up worms crawling over the ground in this search. However, it may come across a crafty worm that is seeking food with its head end while leaving its tail safely in the ground ready for a rapid retreat. In this situation, the badger drills down into the ground after its escaping prey, leaving a characteristic excavation three or four inches deep in the turf called a 'snuffle hole'. Snuffle holes often have a swirl of grasses around the top, dragged round by the badger's nose. They are so called because the badger finds it difficult to breath in this situation, perhaps inhaling soil, and snorting and snuffling as a result.

Other badger signs will be old cow-pats flipped over, or clawed through, whilst searching for *dung beetles* and other insects. Badgers have very long and tough front claws which they use to good effect in this way.

Badgers mark their territories with 'dung pits' – small depressions in which their rather 'loose' droppings, together with secretions from their scent glands, are deposited identifying the owner. The pits are not covered – which would defeat the purpose – and when full new ones are dug thus establishing their boundaries.

Turn right along the hedge at the bottom and walk along to the farm, then walk into the yard through the gate. Please close it after you if you find it shut.

Here, on your right is a range of traditional stone farm buildings with tiles encrusted with lichens and a set of fine steps made from conglomerate stone leading to an upper storey of one of the barns. This stone is often used for steps and I guess it is harder and longer lasting than limestone and less slippery when wet. The buildings here include a cow-shed and open-fronted buildings, few of which are really suited to modern automated agriculture when these days farmers need wide-span multi-purpose buildings into which they can drive tractors, trailers and other machines.

Just before you reach the lane there is a large concrete block on the right, its front edge protected by pieces of metal. It is another relic of a farming practice only recently abandoned; this time connected with the collection of milk. Milk, produced on the farm, was placed in large containers (churns) and left on a churn-stand, such as this one, at a convenient height to be loaded onto the collecting lorry. This vehicle would deliver empty churns and collect full ones before rattling through the lanes to the next farm. Nowadays, the milk produced is stored in a refrigerated tank in the dairy and pumped directly into the bulk milk tanker which calls at the farm every day.

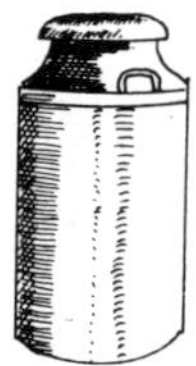

Milk churn

 Turn right into the lane.

A short distance along the lane on your left, a new fence runs at right angles to the road which has been erected instead of the hedge that used to grow here. Hedge removal, either to be replaced by fencing or to enlarge fields for greater convenience when using large machines, has been a frequent occurrence in the past 30 years. Unfortunately, it not only removes suitable habitats for birds, mammals and flowers, but has further depleted the insect population, removing breeding and feeding sites and this has had, in turn, serious consequences for bats.

A little further along, on the other side of the lane, privet can be found in the hedge. This is a shrub most frequently found in southern England and is a member of the olive family. It has dull-green leaves which are not fully ever-green and fall by spring. The privet flower grows in white spikes and has a very sweet scent and the fruit is a black berry containing two seeds. When I walked along here there was an old milk churn in the right-hand hedge. Now that these are no longer required for transporting milk, they have been turned to other tasks and this one seemed to be used to block a hole in the hedge. In the field nearby, a large and fine *willow* tree stands over a field pond. Once a frequent feature of farms, these ponds are also becoming a rarity, depriving populations of amphibians and insects of breeding sites, and causing the *common frog* to become far from common and leading to the protection, by law, of the *great crested newt.*

Magpies, if they detect danger, from an owl or cat perhaps, will mob an animal unmercifully, cackling away in very loud cries.

Here, are often *magpies* – rather smart members of the crow family. With long tails, plumage that is black, white and iridescent blue and a harsh cackling call, they are unmistakable birds that have long been associated with a variety of superstitions. They are true omnivores, eating both insects and seeds, and in spring rob the nests of small birds for the eggs and chicks. Magpies build a domed-shaped nest, a little larger than a football, often constructed with thorny twigs.

Magpies
Piratical collectors of shiny objects

As you round the next bend, there will be a stile before you with two white bars. Climb over it and cross the field aiming slightly to the right of the tall elm stump in the hedge and the church beyond. At the top of the rise in the field you will see the white end of another stile – make for this. Climb the stile and walk towards the church spire.

This spire had great significance in the past for guiding others. The Knoll is clearly visible from the sea and from a distance looks like an island itself. It is claimed that before the Burnham-on-Sea lighthouses were built in 1829 and 1832, the spire of East Brent church was regularly whitewashed to guide ships into Burnham – there is, however, no sign of this now.

As you approach the kissing gate into the churchyard, you will see a number of *sycamore* trees to your left on the boundary between the gate and the field. This is a member of the maple family and was introduced from France in the middle ages. A very quick and successful grower, it has invaded a number of woodlands, taking over as other trees have died or been removed. Unlike the native *oak* which provides homes for other species numbering in excess of 200, the sycamore can provide for a paltry 25 and is considered by many conservationists to be a weed. The tree has distinctive five-lobed leaves, yellowish flowers hanging in clusters and hard brown seeds which grow in pairs and each has a wing on which it twirls as it falls to earth. In spite of its poor reputation, it is very hardy and grows where other trees fail, being successful in habitats ranging from polluted cities to windswept coasts.

Pass through the kissing gate and walk round the church, with its large yews, back down to the village.

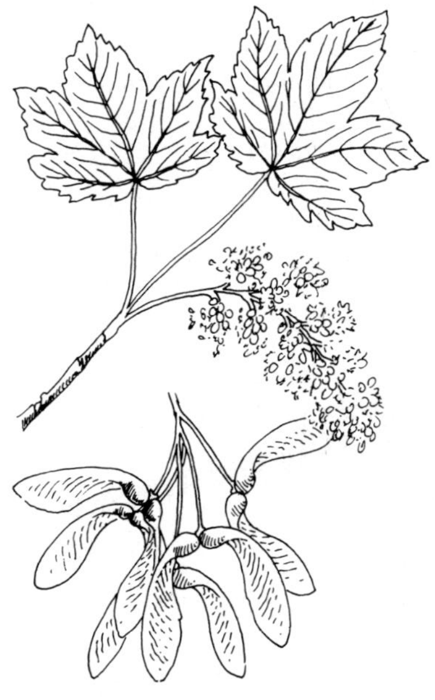

Leaves, flowers and fruit of sycamore

Yew branch and berries

Notes

Notes

Herring Gulls
Steep Holm
Sanderling
Rabbits
Marram grass
Dunlin
Stoat
Fox
Sea buckthorn
Hedgehog
Tide line of sea shells and seaweeds
Ragwort
Reed warbler on common reed

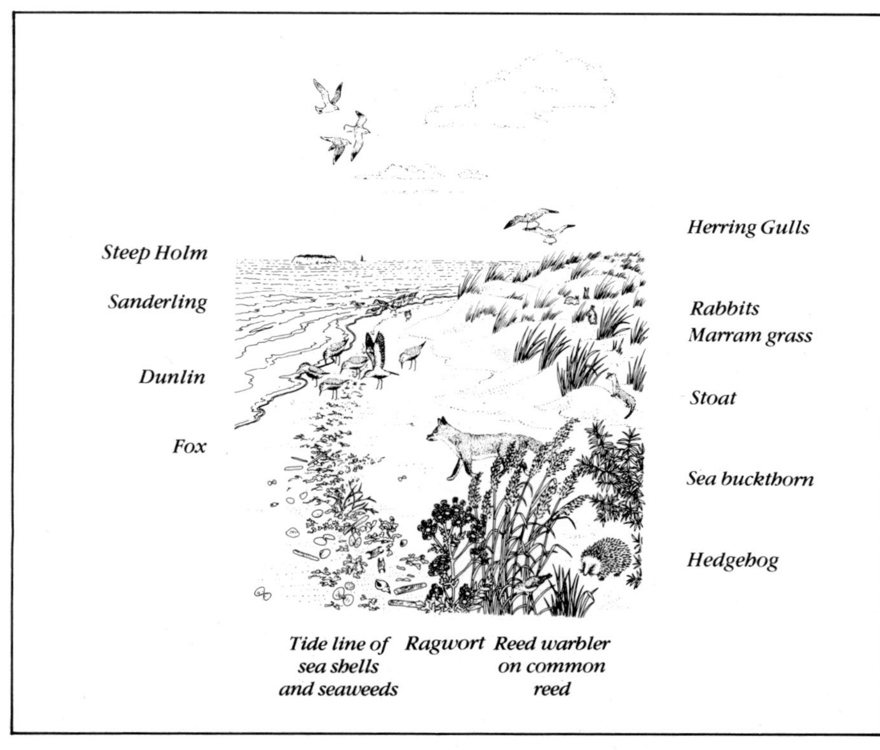

Berrow

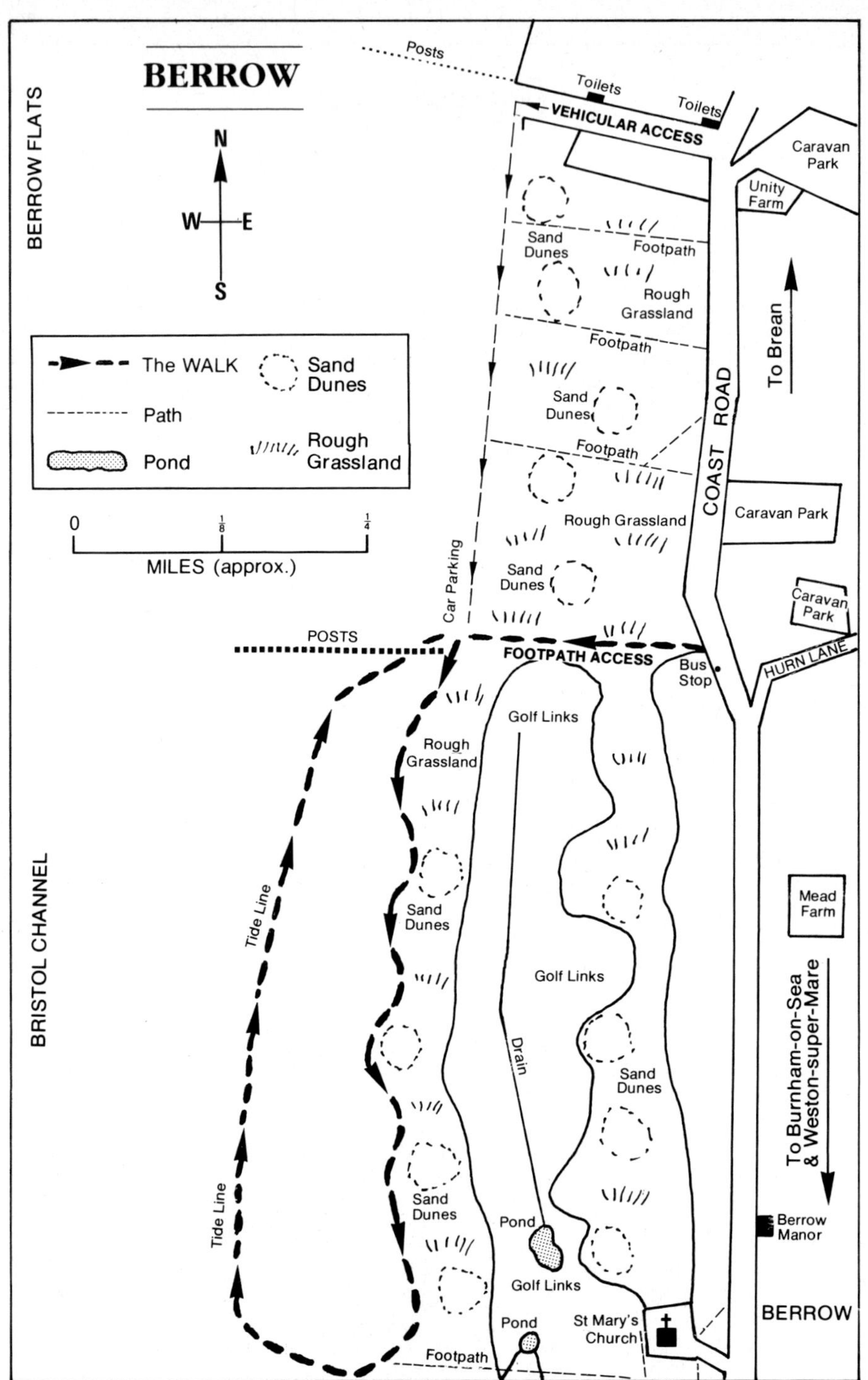
BERROW
N
W
E
S
BERROW FLATS
The WALK
Sand Dunes
Path
Rough Grassland
Pond
0
1/8
1/4
MILES (approx.)
Posts
Toilets
Toilets
VEHICULAR ACCESS
Caravan Park
Unity Farm
Sand Dunes
Footpath
Rough Grassland
Footpath
To Brean
Sand Dunes
Footpath
COAST ROAD
Caravan Park
Rough Grassland
Sand Dunes
Car Parking
Caravan Park
POSTS
FOOTPATH ACCESS
Bus Stop
HURN LANE
Golf Links
Rough Grassland
Sand Dunes
Tide Line
BRISTOL CHANNEL
Mead Farm
Golf Links
To Burnham-on-Sea & Weston-super-Mare
Drain
Sand Dunes
Tide Line
Sand Dunes
Pond
Berrow Manor
Golf Links
BERROW
Pond
St Mary's Church
Footpath

BERROW

O.S. ST25(293534) – Walk on a sandy beach

This is a beach walk of the nicest kind. I have been here when the sand has been almost too hot for bare feet and also when the ice has been piled up on the beach in great parallel banks, each marking a successive tide. The notes for this walk are slightly different from the others in the book. Although I suggest that you keep to the top of the beach on the outward journey and walk back along the tide line, I have not pointed to any specific place to look for any particular species. This is because the area is being moulded all the time by wind and water and changes quickly and easily – in any case, one sand dune looks much like another! I have tried to give a broad guide to things to look for and what you will find depends upon the hour, the season, the weather and your own powers of observation. Although the walk covers about one and a half miles, you can do more if you choose.

If driving enter the beach at the first vehicular access on the left going north, and turn left along the sands. Leave your vehicle at the row of posts which run down the beach (see map). If on foot there is public footpath access opposite Hurn Lane.

One of the most interesting times to visit this beach is early on a spring or summer morning, as this is when animal tracks are at their best (see pages 114–115 for illustrations of some animal tracks). Choose a still morning so that loose sand will not have filled the prints, arrive before other visitors have disturbed the ground, and come when the sun is still fairly low so that its long rays will cast shadows and reveal the form of the tracks.

You will be surprised at the animals which visit the beach. *Foxes* trot through the dunes or walk along the strandline seeking carrion – such as dead gulls washed up by the tide, or the remains of yesterday's picnics – or perhaps they will hunt *rabbits* or smaller mammals. Their fine four-toed tracks make a trail in a line down the sand as if the animal was walking an invisible tightrope. If you follow them you may spot where the fox has sat down on the sand or maybe dug up a rabbit stop: a shallow nursery burrow in which the doe rabbit hides her young. If a predator discovers it, the young rabbits will be excavated and consumed, leaving a small hole and a pile of nesting material. Often the best tracks are made when an animal with sandy feet has walked on mud, as the dry dusty paws leave perfectly-formed prints which, in the case of the fox, show well the long hairs growing between the toes. *Badger* tracks are much broader and have five toes. They have none of the daintiness of those of the fox which, like a dog, walks on tip-toes. Badgers are plantigrade like humans and walk on flat feet, and in mud or damp sand the marks of their long claws, especially those on the fore feet, can be seen very easily.

Badger tracks can be confusing for when walking or trotting, the badger places its hind feet partially or wholly in the tracks of its fore feet resulting in a confusing line of tracks with seven or eight toes to each footprint.

Rabbits come down here too. They like seaside living because of the grasses just inland and the soft sand in which to burrow. Their tracks look a little like a pair of exclamation marks printed sided by side !! and, in spite of first appearances, the rabbit making these would be hopping up the page and not down it. It is quite common to find rabbit skulls among the sand where the animals have been killed or have died of disease (see page 113 for illustrations). The body may have been buried by sand or picked clean by scavengers until only bones remain. The skeleton then breaks up and is scattered, the most recognisable remaining feature being the skull but without the lower jaw. Invariably the base of the skull disappears too, revealing the brain cavity. Look for the small sockets for teeth behind the two incisors – one of the features that distinguishes rabbits and hares from rodents.

Hedgehogs may come down on to the beach leaving a trail of five-toed tracks which look like small human hand prints. These prickly insectivores will look for food of various types and find the soft sand areas especially lucrative as many insects and other invertebrates become trapped in pits in the sand and find it impossible to climb up the tiny moving grains forming the sides. Keep a look out, too, for the delicate trails left by small creatures like caterpillars, beetles, weevils and millipedes.

Two animals you would not expect to find in such a hot dry environment will be the *frog* and the *toad* but, close to Berrow Church, there are ponds on the golf links and fresh water near the top of the beach, and consequently frogs have been found on the sands. Both species leave feathery tracks especially the toad which crawls rather than hops.

At first, the dawn will be chilly and, if you are there before sunrise, you will welcome the warmth it brings as the sun climbs over the horizon and its life-giving glow flows onto the sand. If it is high summer, you may soon wish for the cool of the dawn again as the heat, reflecting off the light-toned sand, turns this place into a mini-Sahara.

The tides ebb and flow in response to phases of the moon. Every month there are spring tides – with a large distance between high and low water – and neap tides – with a much smaller distance. The highest tides of all occur at the equinoxes – around 21 March and 21 September every year.

Common toad – Its warty skin conceals poisonous glands which make it distasteful if bitten

In early summer there will be a surprising variety of plants flowering along the top of the beach and in the dunes. Walk up the gullies, if you leave the beach, and keep off the dune faces, for climbing these can cause serious erosion. The dunes here are held together by the roots of plants growing on them and once these plants are worn away by trampling feet, or the sand around them is removed, the roots lose their grip and the sand, with nothing to hold it, begins to shift. On a windy day it is easy to see this happening and Weston-super-Mare, for instance, acquires sand-drifts on its sea-front roads after an onshore gale. In order to prevent this erosion, many seaside authorities carry out dune-restoration works, these generally come in two parts. The first objective is to slow the wind down for, below a certain speed, the current of air will drop its burden of sand. Many methods have been tried and the most usual is to form a windbreak about two-feet high around which the sand builds up during windy periods. Having got the sand where it is wanted, the second stage is to keep it there and for this *marram grass* is generally used.

Marram is one of three dune grasses which all share similar features for dealing with the conditions imposed by their environment, and all of which are found here. Those dunes nearest the sea are richest in nutrients from decomposing material swept in by the tide and in calcium from pulverised sea-shells.

The rain washes these materials out quite quickly and so the further from the beach, the poorer the growing capacity of the dune sand. At the same time, those dunes nearest the sea are most exposed to salt either carried on the wind or in the form of spray and so greater salt resistance is required by plants growing near the beach. The dunes nearest the sea tend to grow *sea couch grass*, the middle zone supports *lyme grass* and marram grass grows on the so-called 'white dunes' furthest away from the shore.

All three grasses are able to withstand inundation by sand by growing underground shoots which find their way to the surface even after the harshest storm. Marram grass can grow through a metre of sand when necessary. The dry nature of their desert-like home has also led them to evolve ways of conserving water. On hot dry days their leaves roll up to form tubes to prevent loss of moisture, unrolling during damper times when the danger is past.

Another dune-stabilising plant grows here in profusion – the *sea buckthorn* which has a mesh of roots to hold the sand and leathery grey-green leaves to retain moisture. Thorns protect the shrub still further and make it a useful nesting site for small birds. In autumn it produces vitamin-rich orange berries.

A frail-looking yellow flower is also to be found here throughout summer – the *evening primrose* which produces a flower about two inches in diameter on a stem more than two-feet tall. Originally introduced from North America, the evening primrose has spread prolifically on sand dunes and waste areas. True to its name, the evening primrose tends to open on balmy evenings to allow moths to pollinate it.

Marram grass helps bind sand dunes

Evening primrose

Another yellow flower, not exclusively found on dunes and considered by farmers to be a menace, is *ragwort*. Its ragged leaves, from which it takes its name, are the favourite food of the caterpillars of the *cinnabar moth*. The plant is a member of the daisy family and grows up to four-feet tall. It is mildly poisonous to cattle, though not apparently to sheep and certainly not to those caterpillars. These black and yellow-striped larvae will eat the leaves down to the stalk and, having reduced the plant to a skeleton, will climb down to the ground and search for another. The adult moth is generally included among the tiger moths and is a day-flying species. It is crimson and black in colour which probably indicates that it would be distasteful if eaten.

Cinnabar moths and caterpillar on ragwort plant

Along the top of the shore you should also discover *sea spurge* – a typical member of the spurge family whose members are found in many different habitats. It possesses what looks like a green flower which has, instead of petals or sepals, the male and female parts of the plant cupped in bracts which are actually modified leaves.

Near Berrow Church, the tower of which you can see from the beach, are a number of *reed* beds. The reeds themselves look beautiful as their silver feathery heads wave and shimmer in the sun and in spring you may hear *reed warblers* singing from them.

This is as good a place as any to turn round, but you can carry on for a good distance if you wish.

Bridgwater Bay extends to the south and west of you from here and is well known for its profusion of wading birds. These can often be seen feeding at the edge of the incoming tide and a good time to visit is when the tide is creeping in over the broad expanse of mud that forms the estuary of the river Parrett.

Bridgwater Bay is an internationally recognised area for ducks and waders. Its miles of mud flats, which are exposed at low tide and have been declared a National Nature Reserve by the Nature Conservancy Council, attract large numbers of waterfowl especially during migratory periods in spring and autumn.

Sanderling are common, especially in spring and autumn, as many birds use Britain as a stopping-off point to stock up with food when travelling to their Arctic breeding grounds from Africa or vice versa. They are small grey and white birds with a distinctive white wing-bar in flight. Their most common characteristic, however, is their rushing, scurrying behaviour as they dart here and there along the tide line searching for food.

Even more numerous at certain times of the year are *dunlin*, and in February there can be over two thousand here. In summer they can be recognised by their black belly which is a certain give-away while in winter they may be a lot more difficult to differentiate from other species such as the sanderling. They have a longer slightly downcurved bill and a less-pronounced wing stripe in flight. It is when in flight, though, that dunlin come into their own. They have often been compared to a plume of smoke but I find them more mysterious than that. The grey backs and white bellies of their winter plumage make them seem to appear and disappear as if by magic, when they wheel and turn against a white sky, and their aerobatic flight is beautiful to watch.

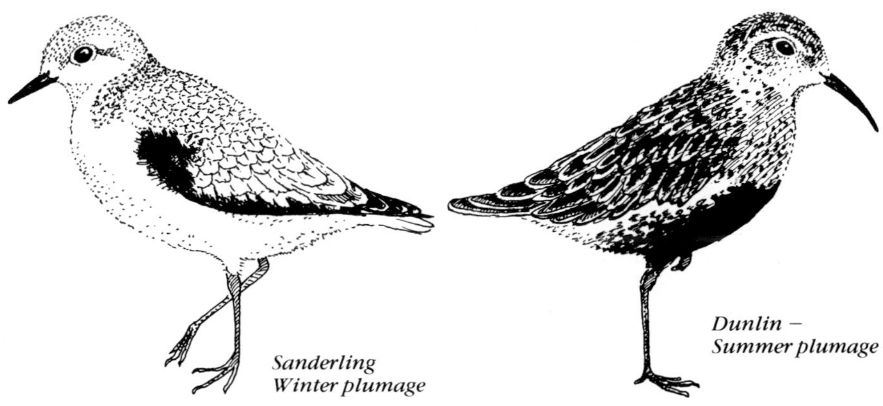

Sanderling Winter plumage

Dunlin – Summer plumage

Two other waders that you may see here are the *curlew* and the *oyster catcher*. The latter is readily distinguishable from other waders by its comparatively large size, its long orange bill, pink legs and black and white plumage which has earned it the nickname of 'sea pie'. They may be in small groups or perhaps just single birds probing in the mud with their beaks. Oyster catchers make a high-pitched 'kleep kleep' alarm call but rarely fly very far if frightened when feeding, landing again a little further along the shore.

When feeding on cockles or mussels oyster catchers either stab or hammer them open. The chicks learn one of these methods from their parents adopting it to the exclusion of the other. The bills of 'hammering' oyster catchers invariably become damaged thus rendering them less effective when seeking other prey.

Oyster catcher

Curlew

Finally there is the curlew, Britain's largest wading bird. It has speckled-brown plumage and an easily-recognisable downcurved bill with which it probes in the mud for food. The bill of the female can be up to one-third longer than that of the male. The other major distinguishing feature is the bird's call of 'coorli' from which it takes its name – a haunting cry which reminds me of wide open marshes or moors, for this bird breeds inland. Like other waders, it nests on the ground laying camouflaged eggs to prevent discovery. Its chicks can leave the nest and run around on the ground with their parents almost as soon as they have hatched. If they feel endangered, the chicks will flatten themselves against the earth, stretching their heads and necks out and keeping still and silent while the parents try to draw the unwanted attentions of the predator away from them.

Walk back along the strand line: the line comprising seaweed and other detritus brought in by the sea and stranded on the beach. The best time to do this is after a storm with an onshore wind, possibly combined with a high tide. You will find all sorts of debris tangled up with the mass of dark weed on the beach; many of the objects are man-made. Wooden items are frequent and may range from a complete fish box to a broom head or the broken handle of a canoe paddle. Increasingly, nowadays, plastics are washed up onto the beach

Shelduck breed in this area. Unlike other duck species, the female is as brightly coloured as the male and so, in order to remain concealed when incubating the eggs, they build a nest underground often in a disused rabbit burrow.

Shelduck

and old bottles, broken toys and bits of fish net are common. Some, like the net, are dangerous and may catch around the legs of a gull or the neck of a seal with fatal results. Such plastic items sometimes carry their own complement of wildlife. I once found a dustbin lid on the beach complete with a small group of ***stalked (goose) barnacles*** attached to its underside. Following a period of south-westerly gales, the lid had arrived, probably from the South Atlantic, with a number of 'passengers'. These animals were still alive, though most of what you will discover during your beachcombing will be skeletons or egg cases.

Common ray (skate)

Goose barnacles

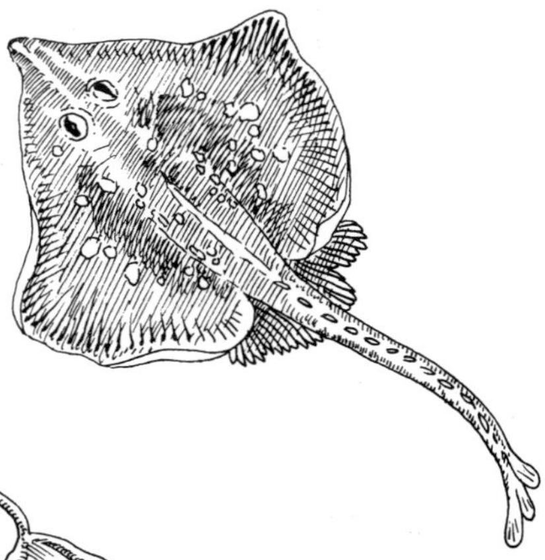

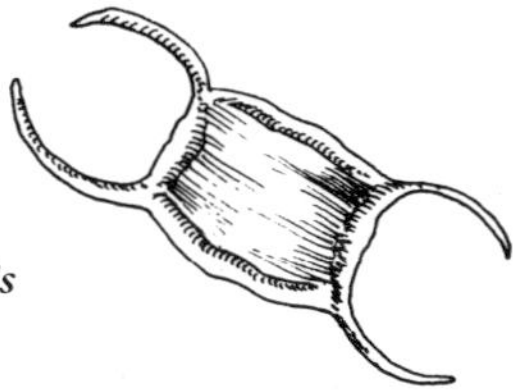

The egg case of the skate has short tendrils and it is known as a mermaid's purse

The majority of animals living on the seashore have exoskeletons: skeletons which, unlike ours, are on the outside of their bodies like crabs, cockles and so on. The bones you will find are in the form of shells and can vary from long *razor shells*, through snail-like *winkle* and *whelk* shells, the shells of *limpets*, to those of *cockles* and *mussels*, which come in matching pairs connected by a hinge of tissue unless broken apart by the waves (see illustrations on page 116). Egg cases are quite common, especially those of the whelk – a light bubbly mass – and of the *skate*, which is a dry dark case with a strand at each corner colloquially known as a mermaid's purse. You may also find a variety of crab shells, or the bone of a *cuttlefish* such as is given to budgies. The really exciting thing about beachcombing is that, like natural history, you never know what might turn up next.

Make your way back to the start.

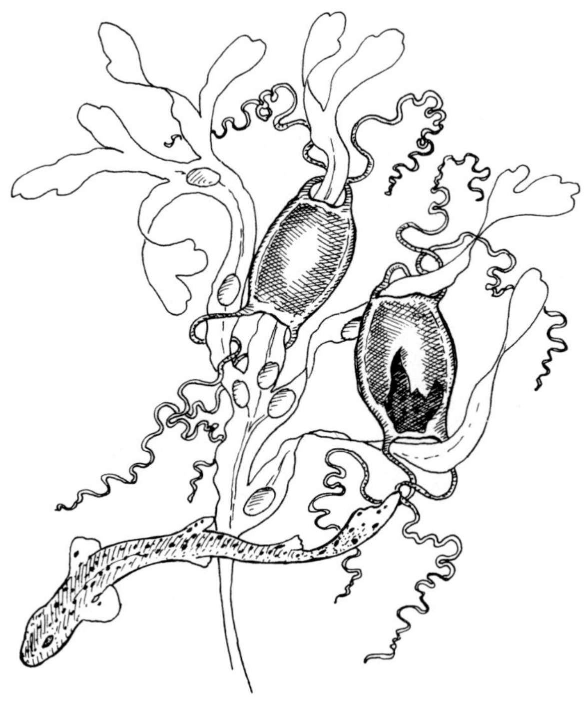

Lesser spotted dog fish egg cases with long tendrils – These are also called mermaid's purses

Notes

Notes

KEYS TO IDENTIFYING WILDLIFE

Unfortunately space does not permit me to include a key to all the species you may see on these wildlife walkabouts. Instead I have set out the following notes on the particular features to look for if you come across a species you do not recognise. These should help you to jot down the important clues which will guide you to a correct identification when you consult your reference books at home or public library. It is difficult to remember colour shades, so to aid with this there is a colour-code chart on the back cover together with a centimetre gauge. It is even better if you can take field guides with you on walks – a flower guide is especially useful as it will help you to resist any temptation to take a sample away with you which, apart from destroying the pleasure of others, is very likely to be against the law. A notebook and pencil is invaluable on any walk.

The following pages contain notes on:

Birds – general identification points
– beak types
– feet types

Plants – general identification points

Ferns – general points
– illustrations

Trees – general identification points
– illustrations of bud, leaf, flower and fruit of horse chestnut tree

Mammals – general identification points
– fur on wire
– hazel nut clues
– skulls and bones
– animal tracks

Sea shells – general points
– illustrations

Insects and Spiders – general rules
– illustrations

BIRDS

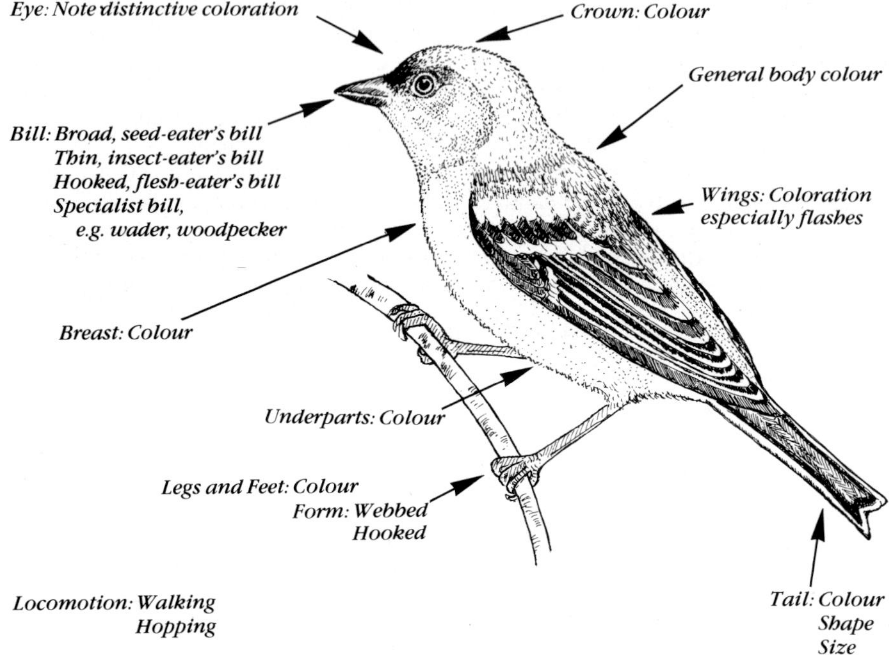

Size: in relation to say a blackbird or starling.

Habitat: where seen e.g. arable land; coniferous woodland.

Activities: feeding on the ground, clinging to tree-trunk, etc.

Time of year.

Area of country.

Sounds: turn them into words if possible e.g. cer-loo (curlew call).

Behaviour: e.g. feeding continuously; short run, feed, short run.

Flight: flight pattern – dipping, hovering, soaring, etc.
speed
altitude
purposeful or localised – hunting insects, fish, displaying, etc.
shape of wings – rounded, pointed, swept back, etc.

Water birds:
swimming and diving for some time
swimming and bobbing under
swimming and upturning with head under and tail in air
diving from branch or air.

BIRDS' BEAKS

Broadly speaking, small birds can be divided into two types by their bills. Those with fine slim beaks are insect-eaters while seed-eaters have broader more powerful bills. There are, however, a large number of specialist feeders who have evolved beaks of a shape suited to their diet. Flesh-eaters have hooked beaks for tearing their prey, waders have long beaks for probing sand and mud, and ducks have flat bills for seiving their food from the water.

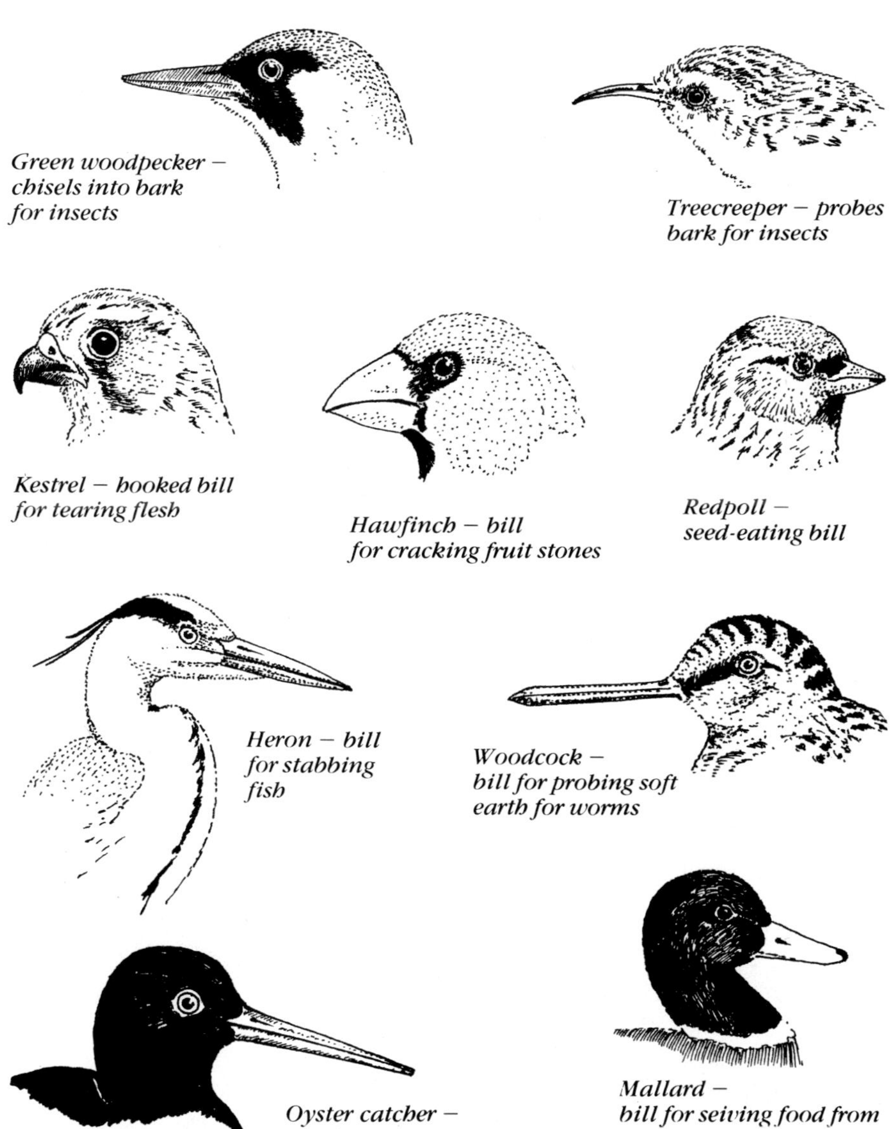

Green woodpecker – chisels into bark for insects

Treecreeper – probes bark for insects

Kestrel – hooked bill for tearing flesh

Hawfinch – bill for cracking fruit stones

Redpoll – seed-eating bill

Heron – bill for stabbing fish

Woodcock – bill for probing soft earth for worms

Mallard – bill for seiving food from water

Oyster catcher – bill for prising open shells

BIRDS' FEET

The more specialist birds have evolved feet to suit their habits and environment, e.g. the webbed feet of water birds which enable them to swim quickly. This specialism tends to make water birds much slower on land and the more aquatic their lifestyle, the less mobile they are out of water and in extreme cases, such as divers, they can hardly walk. At the other end of the scale are coots and moorhens – equally adapted to moving on land and in water. Their feet have lobes on the toes to increase their width when swimming and yet enable them to run unhindered.

Other birds with specialist feet include the predators which have sharp claws for seizing their prey. Woodpeckers have two toes facing forwards and two backwards which allows them to cling to vertical tree trunks with their feet holding the bark in a clamp-like grip.

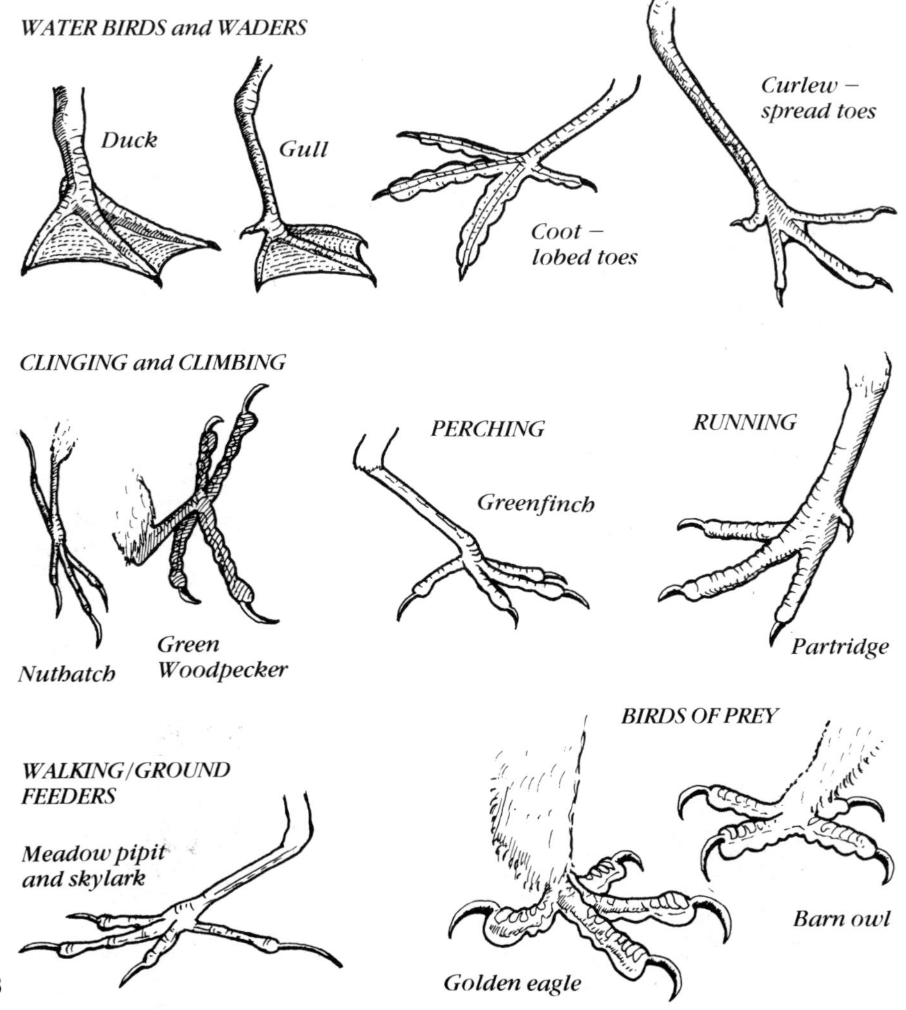

PLANTS

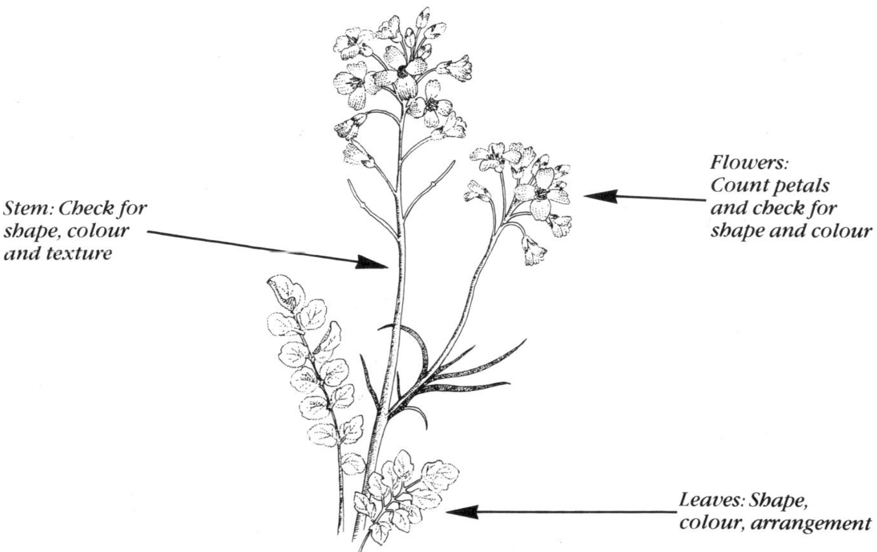

Flowers:
colour: see colour code chart on back cover
general shape: e.g. 'traditional flower'
composite flower like the dandelion
asymmetrical like the foxglove
number of petals, petal shape – rounded, pointed, toothed, etc.
arrangement – single flower on stalk, clustered, several clusters, etc.
size of flower
scent.

Stem:
cross-sectional shape: gauge by feel
texture: smooth, hairy, prickly, etc.
height – see centimetre gauge on back cover
colour

Leaves:
arrangement on stem
edges toothed, saw edged, smooth, convoluted, etc.
veins – prominent, different colour, etc.
peculiar colouration
texture – hairy, dull, shiny, etc.

Seeds: colour, size, how dispersed.

Environment: chalk, limestone area, moorland, etc.

Habitat: hedgerow bottom, stream bank, limestone paving, peat bog, hazel wood, etc.

Time of year.

FERNS

Ferns are primitive flowerless green plants whose ancestors formed present-day coal deposits. On the undersides of fern fronds are brown circular discs which are groups of spore sacs. Either wind or animals disperse the tiny spores, which are released when the sacs split, and from each spore grows a small green disc containing both the male and female parts of the plant. It needs a film of rainwater to enable the sperms to travel to the female egg sacs for fertilisation to occur, and this requirement for a moist climate means that ferns are more common in the humid west of Britain.

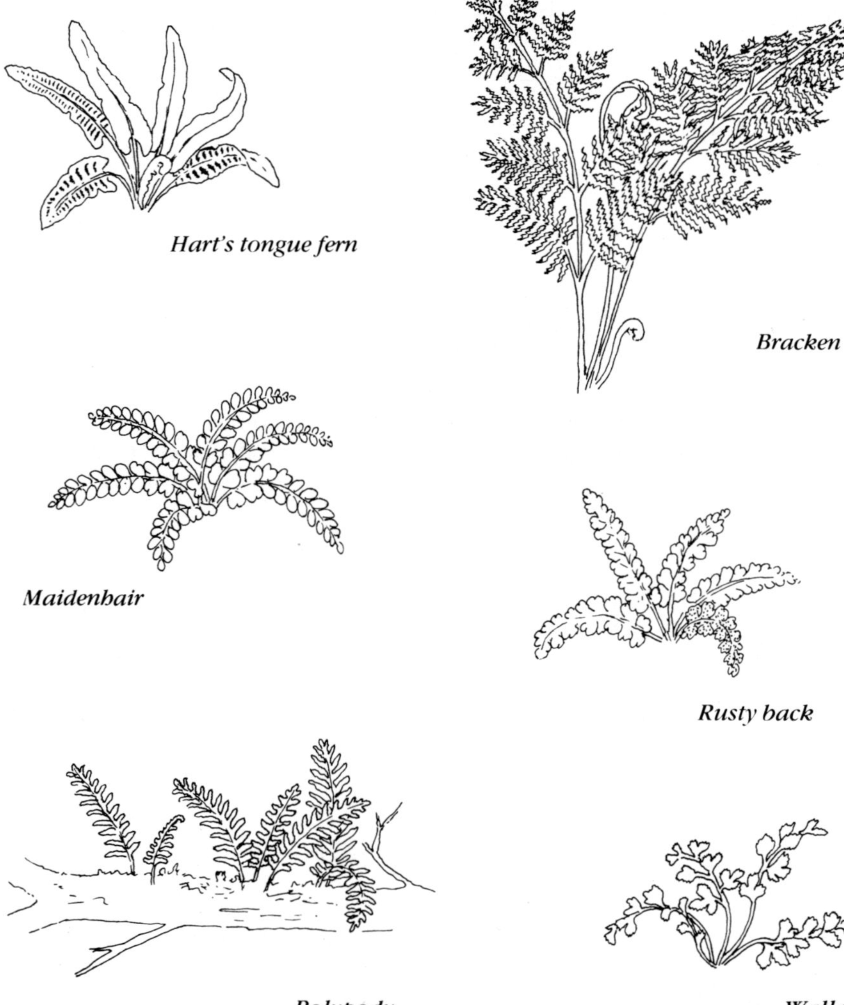

Hart's tongue fern

Bracken

Maidenhair

Rusty back

Polypody

Wall rue

HAZEL NUT CLUES

Small mammals have characteristic ways of opening hazel nuts.

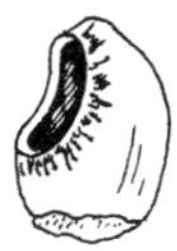

Dormouse

Showing the smooth inside surface to the hole with toothmarks around it on the shell surface.

Bank vole

Showing only corrugated toothmarks around the edge of the hole and no markings on the shell surface.

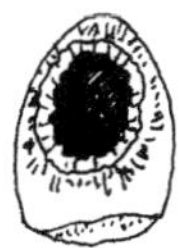

Woodmouse

Showing toothmarks similar to those of the bank vole – around the inside of the hole but with markings on the shell surface as well.

Squirrel

Splits nut into halves along the seam, sometimes nipping the top off first. Young squirrels make quite a mess of a hazel-nut shell when they are first learning the art.

SKULLS AND BONES

Surprisingly few skulls and bones are found in the countryside. Many dead creatures are eaten by scavengers, some of which, like the fox, also remove and hide this source of food. Others are buried by beetles or are covered with leaves or undergrowth. The diggings from badgers' setts are a good place to look as are discarded bottles and owl pellets. You may need a hand lens or magnifying glass to identify the smaller skulls. Skulls make interesting finds and can be readily identified using books on tracks and signs (see bibliography, page 122).

Rabbit skull

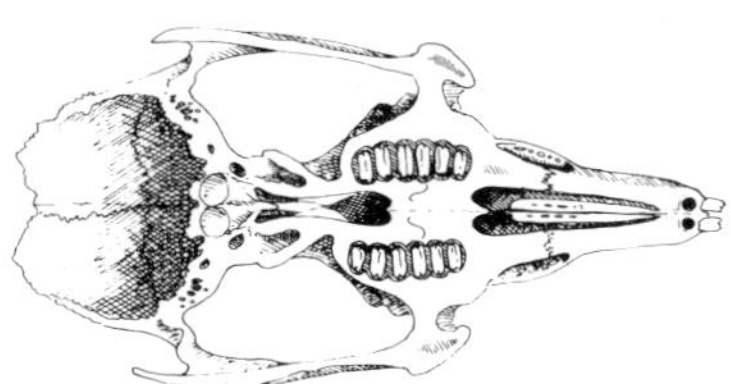

Underside of skull

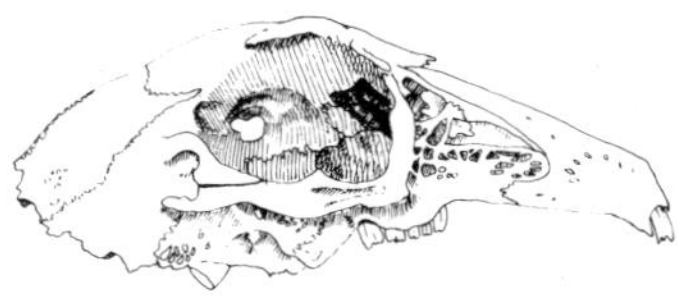

Side view skull, lower jaw missing

ANIMAL TRACKS

The budding nature detective can learn a great deal from animal tracks. Snow is best especially when it is fairly shallow; tracks can be followed for miles if animals have been active during the night. Sand is also a good medium if you arrive before the crowds. Firm mud is fine for recording tracks, either with plaster of Paris or wax – these will not work very well in sand and not at all in snow.

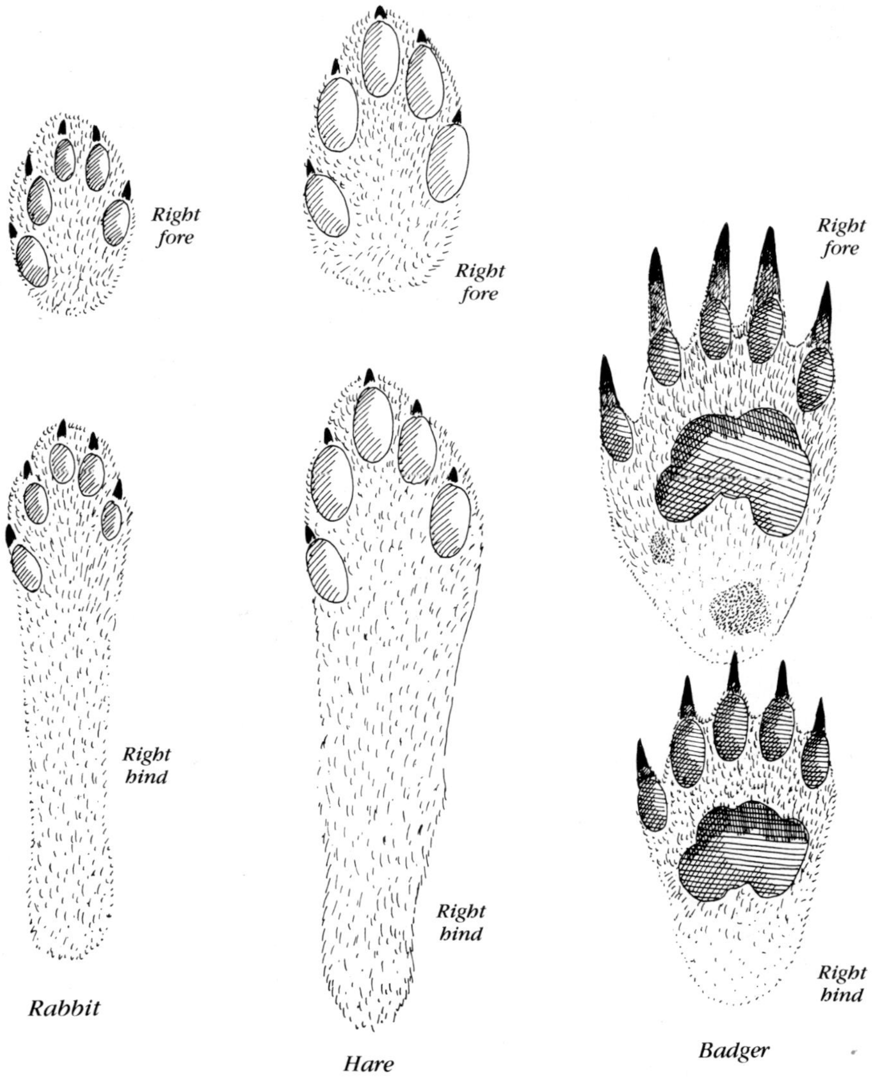

Rabbit

Hare

Badger

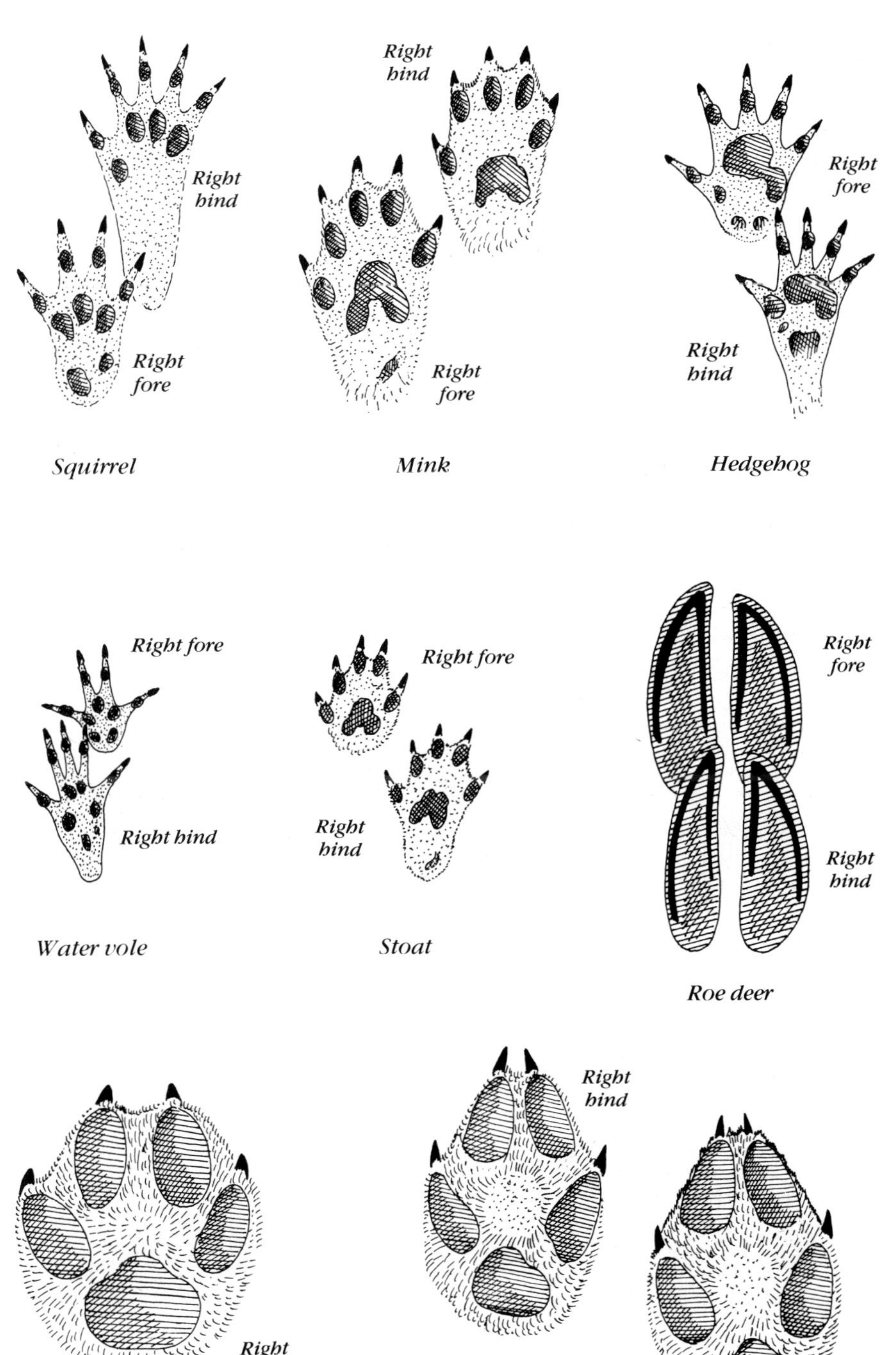
Right hind
Right fore
Squirrel
Right hind
Right fore
Mink
Right fore
Right hind
Hedgehog
Right fore
Right hind
Water vole
Right fore
Right hind
Stoat
Right fore
Right hind
Roe deer
Right fore
Dog
Right hind
Right fore
Fox

SEA SHELLS

Sea shells can be divided into a number of different types. There are those like land snails – the winkle and the whelk; limpets which fasten themselves flat to rocks and move around slowly to feed; and finally there are bivalves which consist of two matching halves. Mussels cling in groups with threads to rocks or pier legs while cockles and razor shells bury themselves more or less deeply in sandy mud.

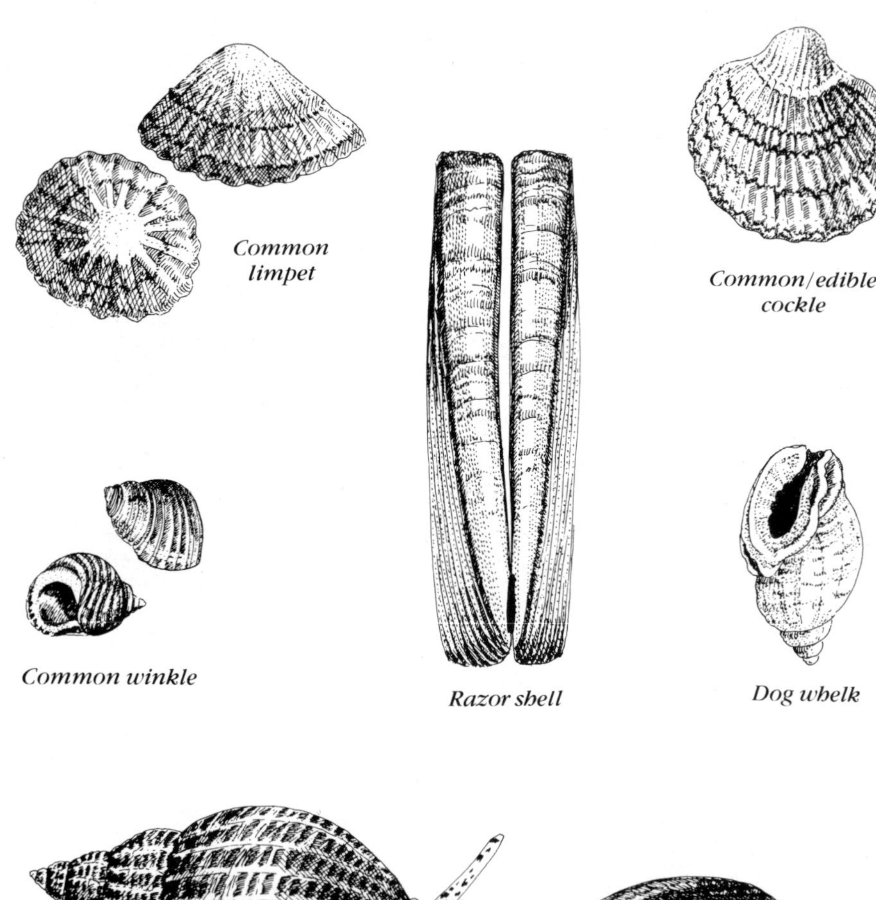

Common limpet

Common/edible cockle

Common winkle

Razor shell

Dog whelk

Common whelk

Common mussel

INSECTS and SPIDERS

General rules:

Insects have:
- 4 wings
- 6 legs
- 2 antennae
- three-part body

The insect class includes:
- beetles
- moths
- butterflies
- dragonflies and damsel flies
- ants and aphids
- bees and wasps
- flies

Bumble bee

Damsel fly

Dragonfly

Spiders have:
- no wings
- 8 legs
- head and body

Spiders belong to a class called *arachnida*, including:
- harvestmen
- scorpions
- mites
- ticks

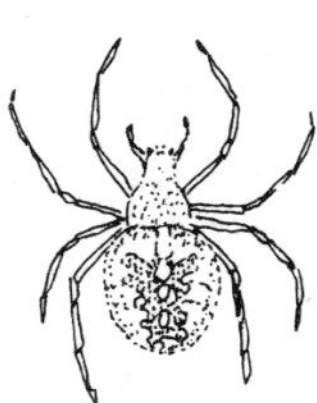

Common garden spider

Notes

COUNTRY CODE

Guard against all risk of fire.

Protect wildlife, wild plants and trees.

Safeguard water supplies.

Keep dogs under proper control.

Go carefully on country roads.

Leave no litter.

Fasten all gates.

Avoid damaging fences, hedges and walls.

Respect the life of the countryside.

Keep to paths across farmland.

WILDLIFE AND THE LAW

Under the 1981 Wildlife and Countryside Act, a large number of species gained special protection. Set out below are some guidelines to the Act.

Plants:
It is illegal to pick some 62 plants and included in this list are many orchids and the Cheddar pink. It is forbidden to dig up any wild plant unless you have the permission of the landowner.

Reptiles and Amphibians:
It is illegal to catch, injure or kill:

the Great Crested Newt	the Sand Lizard
the Natterjack Toad	the Smooth Snake

and it is forbidden to offer for sale any other native reptiles and amphibians.

Mammals:
Some mammals, like the bat and the otter are totally protected so that it is illegal to disturb them and it is even illegal to damage their homes or prevent access to where they live. Other mammals, like the badger, have partial protection which makes it illegal to kill or injure a badger or to be in possession of a live or recently killed badger.

Birds:
The law relating to birds is rather complex and if you need to know the details, the RSPB will help.

If you cause no harm to wildlife and follow the Country Code, you should stay on the right side of the law!

LIST OF ORGANISATIONS

Somerset Trust for Nature Conservation
Fyne Court, Broomfield, Bridgwater, Somerset TA5 2EQ.

Avon Wildlife Trust
209 Redland Road, Bristol 6.

Royal Society for Nature Conservation
The Green, Nettleham, Lincolnshire LN2 2NR.

Royal Society for the Protection of Birds
The Lodge, Sandy, Bedfordshire SG19 2DL.

The British Trust for Ornithology
Beech Grove, Tring, Hertfordshire HP23 5NR.

The Mammal Society
Burlington House, Piccadilly, London W1V 0LQ.

The National Trust
42 Queen Anne's Gate, London SW1H 9AS.

Try your library for a list of local natural history clubs and societies.

BIBLIOGRAPHY

The Natural History of Britain and Europe – (W. H. Smith)

Collins Gem Guides – (Genuine pocket-sized guides) *Wildflowers*, *Butterflies and Moths*, *Birds*, *Trees*, *Wild Animals*, *Mushrooms and Toadstools*

Collins Pocket Guide to *The Seashore* – Barrett and Yonge

Collins Field Guide to: *The Trees of Britain and Northern Europe* – Mitchell
The Birds of Britain and Europe – Peterson, Mountfort and Hollom
The Mammals of Britain and Europe – Van Den Brink

Collins Guide to *Animal Tracks and Signs* – Bang and Dahlstrom

Collins – *The Wild flowers of Britain and Northern Europe* – Fitter, Fitter and Blamey

Mammal Watching – Michael Clark (Nature Watch)

Pond Watching – Paul Sterry (Nature Watch)

Mammals of Britain – *Their Tracks, Trails and Signs* – Lawrence and Brown (Blandford)

Nature Detective – Hugh Falkus (Hienemann)

The Birdlife of Britain – Hayman and Burton (Mitchell Beazley/RSPB)

Trees in Britain, Europe and North America – Roger Phillips (Pan)

Wild Flowers of Britain – Roger Phillips (Pan)

Grasses, Ferns, Mosses and Lichens of Great Britain and Ireland – Roger Phillips (Pan)

INDEX

Italic figures denote illustration.

INDEX

INDEX

Notes

Notes

Notes